Responsive Curriculum Design in Secondary Schools

Meeting the Diverse Needs of Students

Douglas Fisher

Nancy Frey

The Scarecrow Press, Inc.
A Scarecrow Education Book
Lanham, Maryland, and London
2001

SCARECROW PRESS, INC.
A Scarecrow Education Book

Published in the United States of America
by Scarecrow Press, Inc.
4720 Boston Way, Lanham, Maryland 20706
www.scarecroweducation.com

4 Pleydell Gardens, Folkestone
Kent CT20 2DN, England

British Library Cataloguing in Publication Information Available

Library of Congress Cataloging-in-Publication Data
Fisher, Douglas, 1965–
   Responsive curriculum design in secondary schools : meeting the diverse needs of students / Douglas Fisher, Nancy Frey.
      p. cm. — (A Scarecrow education book)
   Includes bibliographical references (p.).
   ISBN 0-8108-4030-8 (pbk. : alk. paper)
   1. Education, Secondary—United States—Curricula. 2. Curriculum planning—United States.
   I. Frey, Nancy, 1959– II. Title.
   LB1628.5 .F57 2001
   373.19′0973—dc21   2001042022

To the teachers and students in the City Heights Educational Pilot
who welcomed us into their classrooms and allowed us to learn about quality instruction.

CONTENTS

ACKNOWLEDGMENTS

Thanking all those responsible for making this book a reality is no easy task. Working as a team prevents anyone from truly "owning" an idea or an innovation. We built on each other's ideas, brainstormed to increasingly more complex levels, and looked to our colleagues for support, constructive criticism, and brutal honesty.

We would like to acknowledge first our editors at Scarecrow Education for believing in us and our ideas and for moving us through the publication process. After we had their support, we turned to the teachers, administrators, and students at the schools we worked with most closely. The administrators who welcomed us into their schools, Emilee Watts, Frank Peterson, and Doug Williams, are phenomenal role models, instructional leaders, and catalysts for change in their schools. Ian Pumpian deserves huge thanks for his role in City Heights and in making this book possible. His belief that together we can make a difference in the lives of our students has been a constant motivating force. He has pushed the boundaries more than anyone we know for creating responsive schools that meet the needs of all students. We would like to give special thanks to our colleagues and friends who provided support and feedback during the writing of this book, including Barbara Bethel, Barbara Buswell, Nancy Farnan, Leif Fearn, James Flood, Cheryl Jorgensen, Diane Lapp, and Caren Sax. This group of amazing individuals we are proud to call friends. And, of course, we must thank all the students who keep us grounded in what works and what needs to be changed in classrooms.

We would also like to thank the artists who contributed to this volume. Loris Marazzi, the Italian wood sculptor, allowed us to use his artwork for the cover. His work can be seen at www.lorismarazzi.com. We would also like to thank Ryan Ott, the graphic artist who created the illustrations for section 3.

Finally, we would like to thank our families for their patience and support during the deadline crunches and the hours of writing and agonizing over details. We are extremely fortunate to have such love.

INTRODUCTION

Advice for many professions includes a provision to know where you want to go so that you'll know when you get there. Teaching is no exception—teachers need to know where to start as they plan their instruction. Most states and districts provide teachers with curriculum framework documents. These documents provide the "what" of teaching, but rarely the "how." Unfortunately, these documents are often only lists of goals that offer little information to teachers who provide instruction to a diverse student population. This book is designed to provide you, the teacher, with a process for designing and implementing curriculum and instruction for your diverse student population.

The first section of this book provides an overview of the responsive curriculum design process. Each of the provided sample lessons was designed by classroom teachers who understood the needs of their students and how to effectively plan instruction. The components of the responsive curriculum design process include addressing the standards; designing multiple assessments; identifying richly detailed source materials, and creating interrelated lessons and culminating activities. The chapters in section one explain each of these processes.

Section two focuses on the needs of diverse learners and how these needs can be addressed while teaching. More specifically, chapter 5 provides an overview of the ways in which literacy can become part of the curriculum. Similarly, chapter 6 discusses various grouping structures that facilitate learning. Chapter 7 focuses on using technology as a learning tool. Finally, chapter 8 addresses the individual learning supports teachers provide to students to ensure they can access the curriculum that has been so thoughtfully designed.

The final section of this book presents a completed instructional plan. This plan focuses on an estuary unit designed for middle school students, but the components of this unit could be adjusted to different content or different grades. The sample is intended to provide readers with a real example of the implementation of the concepts from this book in a classroom with real students.

Section One

Designing Responsive Curriculum

Chapter 1

STANDARDS, EXPECTATIONS, AND ESSENTIAL QUESTIONS

Schools are being held accountable for the achievement of all students, not just those who perform well in traditional educational settings. Data on student achievement underscores the evidence of our failure to make best and emerging educational practices available to all urban youth (Meier, 1995; Sautter, 1994). This impact is most significant in large urban communities (U.S. Department of Education, 1996) because urban districts historically have had student dropout rates of over 40%, and over 70% of students read, write, and compute below grade level (Espinosa & Ochoa, 1992).

The fact is, student achievement among urban youth needs to become a national priority. Focusing on the achievement of all youth is logical and justified, but youth in urban environments deserve increased attention. To many people, the problems and needs of urban America seem insurmountable. It is easy to conjure images of massive poverty, dilapidated private and public structures, crime, vandalism, drug and alcohol problems, child abuse and neglect, and gang fights (Atkins, 1990). Urban and suburban housing and employment patterns continue to result in ethnic and racial segregation and urban unemployment. African-American urban males are more likely to die of gunshot than from any other cause. For many, these urban realities become correlated with the fact that over 75% of urban youth are nonwhite, over 150 languages are spoken in these multiethnic communities, over 15% of urban children are limited English proficient, and enormous disparity exists in the educational achievement curves of urban youth. To people who presume causal relationships in these correlations, urban educational reform appears to be pointless and useless. People who draw such conclusions move if they can, vote for private school voucher initiatives, give up, and, if they do not live there, blame the victims.

Other people, however, are careful to look for ways to tap the strength and resilience existing in these urban settings. They know children can hardly be held accountable for their educational failure when little public equity exists, especially when factors such as the size, age, condition, and resources of school buildings; the amount of per student spending; and the degree of tracking are all negatively represented in the inner cities. The fact that urban children show no marked differences from others when they enter school and progressively fail in comparison after each year of attendance (Sautter, 1994) turns the attention to school and community structures (i.e., policies and practices) and away from a pessimistic deficit view of urban children and the expectations held for them.

People who believe educational reform is possible work hard to bring resources to ideas, ideas to actions, and actions to outcomes. Whether they are involved in building new schools from the ground up with widespread community partnerships or are aggressively challenging traditional tracking, testing, curriculum, or pedagogy, they are demonstrating that change is possible. The reforms that seem most successful in urban settings seem to have a grass roots means of engaging and empowering parents and members of the community to partner with the administrators, teachers, and students of the school.

The teachers whose classrooms we visit in this book are part of the solution. These teachers work in urban environments and focus on a curriculum design process that meets the needs of their diverse student populations. Before we continue, let's take a minute to meet them.

Ms. Monica Kelly teaches fifth grade at Rosa Parks Elementary. She has 34 students, all of whom qualify for free or reduced lunch. Several of her students have recently transitioned from bilingual education classrooms and speak, read, and write in Spanish. She has other students who are learning English at school and speak Hmong, Farsi, or Vietnamese at home. In addition, several students with disabilities who are included in her class also receive support from a special education teacher who provides instruction in the classroom. Ms. Kelly believes in a student-centered classroom. Each table seats four students. Each table has a fish tank on it as well as a box for the group's supplies (tape, scissors, pens, etc.). Students create the room and make all the wall hangings, from word walls, to explorer charts, to class rules.

Ms. Vanessa Scott teaches social studies at Monroe Clark Middle School. She has 30–34 students per period. All of her students qualify for free or reduced lunch and receive sheltered instruction because they are also English language learners and speak a second language at home. She teaches as a member of a "house," a group of four team teachers who all have the same students. Ms. Scott enjoys hands-on activities that capture her students' interests. She also likes to develop integrated curriculum units with the other members of her team.

Mr. Jeff Simon also teaches at Monroe Clark Middle School. He teaches seventh and eighth grade science to 30–34 students per period. Like Ms. Scott, Mr. Simon works in a "house" with a team of teachers. Mr. Simon believes that teachers must develop powerful relationships with students in order for them to learn. His classroom is a place where students know they will be respected. His students also know that they have to read, write, and learn every day in his class. Like his colleagues, Mr. Simon has a range of learners in his class, including students with disabilities who receive special education services.

Ms. Cristina Gutierrez teaches English to ninth graders at Hoover High School. She is a recent graduate of the San Diego State University teacher credential program and was hired at the school where she did her student teaching. As in other urban schools, Ms. Gutierrez's students qualify for free or reduced lunch and are diverse in terms of ethnicity, exceptionalities, and experience with school. Ms. Gutierrez loves literature and wants all of her students to love literature as well. She knows that the modeling she provides her students is key to their development.

The Role of Curriculum and Curriculum Design

Curriculum has been described in many ways (Posner, 1995). Some people talk about curriculum as the content that is covered in a specific class. Others maintain that curriculum is also the instructional strategies that teachers use. We use the term curriculum to describe a course of study. In other words, we view curriculum as both the content and methods a teacher uses to plan and conduct his or her class. This book focuses on the content of the curriculum and the ways in which teachers ensure that all students access the core curriculum. However, before we can turn to a discussion of responsive curriculum design, we must first examine the standards and expectations that are established for all students.

Standards

The national effort to improve the educational achievement of America's school children is grounded in the establishment of rigorous learning standards at every level of elementary and secondary education (Roach, 1999). In developing a standards-based system, policymakers and educators hope to refocus teaching and learning on a common understanding of what communities expect students to know and be able to do as a result of their public school experience (Tucker & Codding, 1998). Once established, the standards provide the foundation for deciding what to teach and how to assess students' progress.

Curriculum frameworks are outlines that establish benchmarks for curriculum content at the various grade levels, thus providing the broad context from which districts then develop their specific curricula. These benchmarks become the goals and objectives that students should meet in each grade level. In some states, these frameworks merely provide voluntary guidance to local districts as they develop their curriculum. In other states, the frameworks provide the foundation for new statewide assessment systems, as well as guidance for textbook approval, curriculum priorities, and instructional strategies.

The proponents of standards-based reform maintain that if high, rigorous standards are created for all students and clearly communicated to educators, students, family members, business leaders, policy makers, and the community at large, then a coordinated effort can be mounted that focuses on increased achievement (National Association of State Boards of Education [NASBE], 1996; Tucker & Codding, 1998). The intended result is that all students, from all socioeconomic backgrounds, those with limited English proficiency, and students with disabilities, will achieve (McDonnell & McLaughlin, 1997). In other words, the expectations for all students are increased, and the entire system is focused on helping students achieve those higher expectations.

Types of Standards

Several types of standards are used in schools today. Most commonly, *content* standards refer to the specific curriculum for a specific class. Often these are developed at the district or state level. For example, a class called "algebra" has specific competencies that students are expected to master if they receive credit in the class. The content standards do not provide teachers with guidance for planning instruction, but do provide teachers with information about what should be taught.

In addition to the content standards, *performance* standards are often developed at the district or site level to ensure that students can demonstrate their knowledge across traditional academic disciplines. The Hoover Learner Outcomes (HLOs) listed here are an example of performance standards. Notice that most of these standards could be demonstrated across classes and subject areas. They also allow teachers from different disciplines to talk about their expectations for students beyond the curriculum.

Hoover Learner Outcomes

1. The student will demonstrate **habits of inquiry and knowledge** in the following ways:
   - Demonstrates creativity by asking essential questions using habits of mind—evidence, connection, supposition, and significance
   - Distinguishes and states fact from opinion and/or acknowledges differing points of view
   - Demonstrates scientific inquiry by posing research questions, conducting research, and supporting decisions and solutions to problems with evidence
   - Demonstrates mathematical logic, reasoning, and cause-and-effect relationships through problem solving
   - Demonstrates the ability to apply decisions or solutions to future situations by making predictions, connections, and/or recommendations
   - Demonstrates subject matter knowledge through the use of inquiry and through evaluation or interpretations that are substantiated by examples or data from the discipline
   - Uses appropriate electronic sources, including the Internet and CD-ROMs, to research, interpret, and process information
2. The student exhibits **habits of work** in the following ways:
   - Plans and organizes time, money, people, or materials with written evidence of completing a project, event, or set of goals
   - Demonstrates the ability to handle real-life issues in finance, time management, study habits, and day-to-day living
   - Demonstrates the ability to collect, analyze, and organize resources and information
   - Shows accountability to the group by following through on commitments, schedules, responsibilities, and meets deadlines to achieve a shared goal or the needs of a client
   - Documents different roles by establishing and operating self-directed work teams
   - Evaluates self and peer performance in a group
   - Demonstrates the use of computer platforms and a variety of software applications, including word processing, to compile, edit, polish, and preserve work
   - Cites a variety of primary and secondary sources to validate research or to support a project
   - Uses statistics to make generalizations from data
   - Maintains a portfolio of selected work and achievements exhibiting the Hoover Learner Outcomes

3. The student will **communicate ideas and information** in the following ways:
   - Uses standard English in a variety of writing types and in verbal communication
   - Uses the language of mathematics to communicate ideas and concepts and to explain reasoning and results
   - Writes and speaks with clarity and with a sense of purpose
   - Evaluates, corrects, and revises written, verbal, or other forms of communication
   - Demonstrates listening, reading, and observational skills through written, verbal, and other types of responses
   - Designs presentations and performances using organization, content, and visuals appropriate to the audience
   - Selects appropriate graphics, charts, fonts, sounds, music, video, and other design elements for publications and presentations
   - Teaches new skills and ideas to others while giving and receiving constructive feedback

4. The student will **plan for the future and show a commitment to lifelong learning** in the following ways:
   - Identifies and addresses career and personal priorities through the development of educational, career, and personal plans
   - Seeks new information and understanding by exploring career opportunities through research, job shadows, and internships
   - Demonstrates awareness and understanding of post high school educational options and career choices
   - Shows involvement and participation in fitness and recreation and demonstrates the importance of these activities as part of an ongoing fitness program
   - Shows self-awareness of leisure choices and how these choices connect to lifelong plans
   - Gives service to the school and outside community
   - Uses technology that is relevant to the workplace and demonstrates understanding of common terms associated with technology
   - Participates in voter registration

The Impact of Standards-Based Reform

What is the impact of the standards-based reform initiative on students in urban schools? Intuitively, many people think that increasing educational standards ought to benefit all students. As it concerns students with diverse learning styles, parents and educators have long believed that raising expectations results in higher achievement. Educators often imagine that if our local school officials want to increase the percentage of students who score in the "proficient" or "mastery" categories on state assessments, they will want to increase all students' access to rigorous academic classes and effective teachers. We are encouraged by the thought that adopting higher expectations for students would lead to the dissolution of remedial classes such as "Applied English," "Functional Math," and "Science Skills." Perhaps even greater numbers of students in urban schools might be enrolled in college preparatory classes, thus broadening their career options and their potential earning power as adults.

Furthermore, educators understand that adopting high standards for all students should promote the elimination of tracking and the inclusion of students with disabilities more fully in the mainstream of general education based on common learning standards for all students (Fisher, Sax, & Pumpian, 1999). In the context of standards-based reform, the curriculum is viewed as a unifying vehicle to ensure that a variety of students "master" the same information.

There is, unfortunately, another less positive scenario for describing the impact of standards-based reform on students who have traditionally been marginalized—students who qualify for Title 1 programs based on their family income, English language learners, students with disabilities, and students in migrant education programs. What if states develop learning standards that do not reflect the needs of these students or others who traditionally have been only marginally included in the educational system? What if different standards are developed for different kinds of students—honors expectations for honors students, special education expectations for special education students, etc.? If all students are not considered in the development of general standards or the design of curriculum frameworks, or if their test scores are not included in an aggregate district score, an even more segregated system of education might evolve. It is possible that schools would do more tracking, and some students would have less access to high-level curriculum than they do now. Fewer students might graduate with a high school diploma, and their future educational and career choices would continue to be limited.

Responsive Curriculum Design

Determining what and how to teach all students—the content of the curriculum—requires that we examine more than just the body of knowledge that currently exists in particular academic disciplines. All students need to learn three types of skills.

- Content area knowledge (in science, social studies, language arts, math, computers, the arts, etc.)
- Dispositions, social skills, and habits of mind (such as inquisitiveness, diligence, collaboration, work habits, tolerance, and critical thinking)
- Communication skills such as reading, writing, speaking, and listening

Educators concerned primarily with teaching students with diverse learning needs might wish that all schools would develop their curriculum—the content of what they teach—to address all three of these skill areas. If they did, it would be possible for any school to address any student's priority learning goals. No school would be "too academic," "too vocational," or "too devoted to the basics." And this could be accomplished by setting high standards for all.

Considering the variability in curriculum and instruction from district to district and school to school, we recommend that all teachers use some common curricular elements to design teaching/learning experiences that transcend philosophical differences and result in a learning environment that challenges and supports all students (see figure 1.1).

Figure 1.1   Responsive Curriculum Design

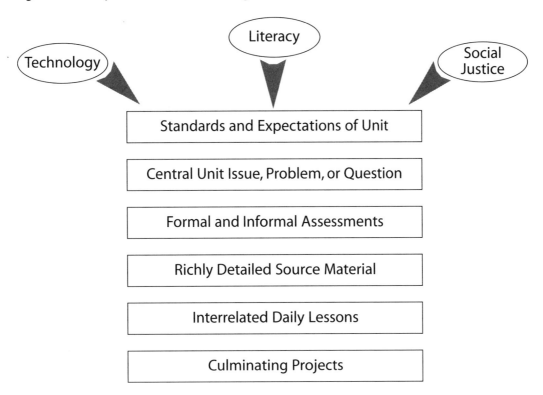

In addition to identifying the academic, communication, and social objectives you have for the unit, you will need a way of communicating the overall focus of the unit to students. We suggest structuring a unit of study around an issue, problem, or essential question. This creates a framework for the learning experience and provides direction and coherence (Jorgensen, 1994). In a standards-based curriculum, teachers generate these "central unit" issues with the standards firmly in mind. In an ancient civilization unit, for example, the issue might be "Are the Greeks still with us today?" In this unit, students can demonstrate their mastery of several content standards, depending on the particular activities and products the teacher has planned. Students can illustrate that they understand the concepts of continuity and change in history, as well as principles and processes of social systems (such as the Olympics). They also should be able to comprehend and assess the content and artistic aspects of oral and visual presentations.

The question posed in a unit of instruction should not be one that can be answered with a simple "yes" or "no" or some other one-dimensional response. The question is not raised because the teacher already has a single "correct" answer in mind. Rather, the question should challenge each student to discover his or her own unique answer. The question "What is a hero?" can serve to focus an interdisciplinary study on today's media portrayals of sports, political, and entertainment heroes, as well as examining why other heroes, such as those who contribute to their communities, are often overlooked. The use of an overarching central question can challenge students' ability to consider the complexities posed by many of the challenging issues in today's world.

Central unit issues, problems, and questions serve as a way of focusing the teacher's planning as well. The use of this "backward planning" approach (McTighe & Wiggins, 1999) allows the teacher to articulate to students exactly what the outcome of the unit will be. The culminating projects for the unit should include opportunities for students to respond to the question or problem first posed in the unit.

When all students in a classroom are focused on addressing a common question, differences in learning style and ability are less important than the commonality of all students constructing meaning in the content area, albeit in a personalized way. Well-crafted "essential questions" or problems offer challenge and accessibility to all students.

When the entire school is focused on essential questions at the same time, students can discuss their thinking about these questions during passing periods, at lunch, and at other social times. This creates a schoolwide conversation about the overarching curriculum goals. For example, at Pojoaque Middle School the essential question "What is a hero?" was plastered around the school, placed on book covers in the library, read in the daily bulletin, and posted on the marquee for the community to see. We had evidence that the curriculum from this middle school became a community focus when we heard a waiter ask a group of students after school one day, "So what do you think about heroes now?"

Standards in the Classroom

Thus, the first step in responsive curriculum design is to identify the standards and expectations for the unit of study. Teachers identify specific content, social, and communication expectations for students from the state and local standards, the school's performance standards, and an understanding of the communication and social needs of children and young adults.

For example, in Ms. Kelly's fifth grade classroom, students were expected to understand the economic forces that led to the need for world exploration. She also wanted her students to understand the life of explorers, where explorers came from and where they went, and the variety of technological advances that made exploration of "the New World" possible.

In Ms. Scott's seventh grade world history class, she began with the question "How are archaeologists able to reconstruct meaning of the past based on artifacts?" Ms. Scott used this question to address her core social studies standard, "to differentiate between facts and historical interpretations by examining historical data, documents, narratives, and artifacts, and assessing their credibility and identifying bias." In addition to this content standard, Ms. Scott wanted her students to speak and write about their understanding of archaeologists' roles. Further, she addressed a social expectation for her students—their ability to work in a group.

Ms. Gutierrez's ninth grade English class focused on the novel *Goodbye, Vietnam* as part of a grade-level focus on "knowing yourself through others." The standards addressed in this unit included the students ability to perform the following activities:

- Evaluate, interpret, summarize, and make connections through literature circles, shared reading, read alouds, and journal responses

- Make predictions, infer information, and think beyond reading assignments
- Express thoughts and ideas using literature circles, journals, and visual representations
- Explore characters, setting, plot, climax, and themes in literature
- Gain a deeper understanding of characters through analysis of self
- Develop reading comprehension skills by using Post-it® notes to mark important quotes/statements, identify literary symbols, construct open-ended questions, and unknown vocabulary meanings
- Develop Internet search skills

Each of these teachers first considered the standards and expectations of the unit they wanted to plan. This first step allowed them to focus the unit, allocate instructional time for the unit of study, and plan instructional activities. Throughout this book, we return to these three classrooms as we outline the responsive curriculum design process. In addition to these three classrooms, the third section of this book contains a completed unit plan that may be useful in reviewing the curriculum design process.

Chapter 2

DESIGN MULTIPLE FORMAL AND INFORMAL ASSESSMENTS

The keystone of effective assessment is the teacher's ability to articulate how students can demonstrate what they have mastered. What evidence will be accepted to show that each student has met the content and performance standards identified for the unit? Educators have long recognized that paper and pencil tests alone rarely provide students with the opportunity to show what they know, yet these assessments are sometimes done to the exclusion of richer performance-based assessments. And students with diverse learning styles may not always respond favorably to assessment methods that mine only verbal-linguistic and mathematical forms of intelligence.

Intelligence is comprised of many different kinds of abilities and talents (e.g., Gardner, 1999). While teachers historically emphasized verbal-linguistic and logical-mathematical intelligences to the exclusion of most other talents, teachers in responsive curriculum classrooms design instructional and assessment activities that tap into the multiple forms of intelligence possessed by all students. In this model, students have a range of ways to demonstrate what they know. For example, in a unit on inventions that utilizes all of the students' intelligences, musically inclined students study the science behind the invention of electronic music; "spatially smart" students build or draw a new invention; and students with strong linguistic and interpersonal intelligence form a discussion group and write "policy briefs" on the use of inventions that are intended to cause harm, such as the atomic bomb. These performance-based projects serve as a means of assessing the depth of knowledge a student has acquired while participating in the unit.

This provision of varied opportunities to demonstrate mastery carries a corresponding necessity to utilize multiple forms of assessment. To ensure powerful student learning, teachers monitor and assess students' progress throughout the unit, not just at the end. The greater diversity found in the classroom makes the need for periodic assessment critical. For these reasons, multiple assessments are important elements of responsive curriculum design. In order to strategically utilize assessments, an understanding of the types and purposes of assessments is required.

Types of Assessments

Formal Assessment

Assessments can be categorized into two broad fields: *formal assessments* and *informal assessments*. Tests that require a traditional, paper-and-pencil response to a series of questions with a clearly "correct" answer are often considered to be formal assessments. Formal assessments share a fundamental construct—they measure student responses by comparing or referencing a particular exemplar. The exemplar they reference governs whether the test is *norm-referenced* or *criterion-referenced* (see figure 2.1). Norm-referenced tests measure a student's responses to a set of questions by comparing, or referencing, the scores of a group of similar students from other geographical locations (Flood, Lapp, & Wood, 1997). These instruments, also called standardized tests, are most commonly administered at regular intervals to large groups of students. For example, the SAT-9 is the norm-referenced test currently being used in California. Criterion-referenced tests differ from norm-referenced tests because the exemplars in criterion-referenced tests are specific instructional objectives or standards. Large-scale criterion-referenced tests have been developed by some states to measure student progress on state standards (e.g., Florida Comprehensive Achievement Test, Michigan Educational Achievement Test). A more common application of criterion-referenced testing is the chapter test, given to students after the completion of instruction on a unit.

Both norm-referenced and criterion-referenced tests have limitations. Norm-referenced tests are most useful as a very broad measure of competency (Stanley & Hopkin, 1972). A student's results on a standardized achievement test like the SAT-9 can document progress in content areas compared to other students around the country (Popham, 1999). However, it lacks the precision to diagnose a student's areas of weakness and strength within a content area (Lapp & Flood, 1992). Another limitation of norm-referenced tests is the restriction of the test items themselves. No single test could hope to query students on the entire body of knowledge contained in science, for example. Therefore, the test designers must limit the questions to a sampling of the content. Consequently, a student's performance on such a test is influenced by how closely the test design corresponds to that student's in-school and out-of-school science experiences.

Criterion-referenced tests also have shortcomings. The validity and reliability of a criterion-referenced test is dependent on how clearly the behavioral objectives are defined and how well the test item measures that behavioral objective. Straightforward facts like being able to name the five Great Lakes of the United States are easy to assess. But assessing a student's understanding of the influence of these large bodies of water on the economic development of the region is more difficult to measure. A test maker is left with two equally unappealing choices: reduce the desired answer to the latter question to a simplified and easily measured response, or skip the item altogether in favor of the former question. Both choices challenge the test maker's ability to measure a student's higher order critical thinking skills.

Figure 2.1   Formal and Informal Assessments (adapted from Flood, Lapp, & Wood, 1997).

Formal Assessment Type	Purpose	Procedure
Standardized Tests (Norm-Referenced)	to measure a student's performance in a variety of skills and compare those scores to students in other geographic locations	administered at set intervals; students answer questions from booklet on standard forms
Criterion-Referenced Tests	to indicate attainment of mastery on specific instructional objectives, usually by answering a percentage of questions correctly	administered with lesson plans; students read items and answer on separate paper
Teacher-made and Publisher-made Tests: True/False, Fill-in, Multiple Choice	to measure retention and comprehension of specific content	administered within lesson plan; students answer focused questions in various formats

Informal Assessment Type	Purpose	Procedure
Observations	to assess a student's use of language in a variety of instructional settings	observe and record student's use of language, often written in logs or journals
Skills Checklists	to track a student's development by noting which skills have become or are becoming part of a repertoire	set up a checklist of desirable skills in language arts and periodically observe the student to determine which have been attained
Rubrics	to evaluate students by comparing their work to a pre-established set of criteria	share rubric with students, collect student work and compare to rubric, share results with students with specific feedback
Portfolio Assessment	to document in a variety of ways how a student has developed as a language user	teacher collects or student selects samples of work, including "published" writing, taped oral readings, conference notes
Conferencing	to provide opportunities for the teacher and student to discuss development	student and teacher meet at set times to review performance and discuss instruction that may be required for student to progress
Peer Reviews	to involve students in the evaluation process and to build their evaluative and interactive skills	give students guidelines for evaluation; two or more meet to discuss one another's work, peer's grade is factored into final grade
Self-Assessment	to empower students by making them responsible for and reflective of their own work	students continually evaluate their performance and progress via checklists, interactions, inventories, conferences, and portfolios

Informal Assessment

In an era during which the broadly collected data from standardized tests is being used to make far-reaching educational decisions about large groups of students, it is vital that informal assessments also be recognized for their contribution to what is known about an individual student. Far more than standardized test results, which often do not arrive until the following school year, informal assessments are the tools educators rely on in daily instruction. *Informal assessments* are those selected and administered by the classroom teacher in order to determine what instruction needs to occur next. Astute classroom teachers possess a wealth of information about their students' knowledge of literacy and content and evaluate events such as book talks, classroom discussions, and permanent products to gauge students' progress and drive future instruction. Wise practitioners recognize the value of such informal assessments as a rich source of data.

Informal assessments differ from formal assessments because they do not require the systematic procedures for administering tests and interpreting test results (Leslie & Jett-Simpson, 1997). Many informal assessments are constructed by the teacher in an effort to measure a specific aspect of the curriculum. These informal assessments often consist of observations, skills checklists, portfolio assessments, conferencing, peer reviews, and self-assessments (see figure 2.1). Each category is discussed separately.

Seven Assessments for Responsive Curriculum Development
Observations

As students work in the classroom, teachers observe them and gain information about their knowledge and strategies. Sometimes these observations occur in unlikely settings, like on the playground or during an assembly. At other times, a teacher may deliberately construct a task in order to observe a student's response. Teachers frequently identify observations as the most important source of information about students (West, 1998).

Yetta Goodman (1985) coined the term "kidwatching" to describe how astute teachers collect information about student performance. This is often accomplished through the use of anecdotal records—brief notes about a student's responses. Recording observations can be as simple as using a clipboard with Post-it® notes in order to jot quick notes about a student's academic or social behavior. These notes are later added to a binder of pages, one for each student. Over time, the teacher can analyze these anecdotal records for patterns. Although teachers cannot possibly begin to document all their observations, documentation on some occasions can assist reflection and sharing information with students, parents, administrators, and the next year's teacher. Telling a parent that his or her child has a difficult time contributing to book club discussions becomes more meaningful when the teacher's notes show that the child failed to participate in the group on three of the five observed occasions.

There are several guidelines for creating and maintaining anecdotal records to increase their usefulness. Many teachers favor using an anecdotal record form of their own creation. It is advisable to include the name of the student, the date, duration of the observation, and a description of the observed task data that are beneficial when later analyzing

Figure 2.2   Anecdotal Record Form

Name of Student: _____   Begin Time: _____

Date: _____   End Time: _____

Group Arrangement

Individual: _____

Partner: _____

Small Group: _____

Whole Class: _____

Description of Observed Task:

Observations:

the information gathered over several observations. See figure 2.2 for an example of an anecdotal record form.

A teacher may also construct an observational event in order to elicit student responses for the purposes of informing future instruction. An example of this is the KWL (what do we know/what do we want to know/what have we learned) chart (Ogle, 1986). When a sixth-grade teacher used a KWL at the beginning of a social studies unit on Ancient Egypt, he discovered that his students were interested in finding out about the lives of women and children in various social classes. He then applied this observational data by including the books *Growing Up in Ancient Egypt* (David, 1993) and *Women in Ancient Egypt: The Other Half of History* (MacDonald, 1999) into the readings his students would use to answer the central question, "Would you survive in ancient Egypt?" Observational assessment was also done at the end of this unit using the KWL chart. The last phase, "what I learned," was done first in small groups, then completed in a class-wide discussion. The teacher recognized that this instructional event served the multiple purposes of reinforcing new knowledge and providing him with a window on the progress of the class.

Skills Checklists

Checklists can also be helpful tools for documentation because they allow teachers to specify particular dimensions for observation and provide a means for summarizing those observations. Teachers may use a checklist to serve as a simple instrument for capturing students' evolving listening, reading, speaking, and writing skills. Many checklists are available in the literature on literacy practices (e.g., Clay, 1985; Harp, 1994; Ruddell, 1991; Sulzby, 1991). Checklists can also be designed to focus on a particular aspect of literacy instruction, such as a book club. The teacher can "listen in" to a book club discussion to note the strategies being used by readers in their effort to make meaning of the text. For example, an observation using a checklist of notable features of a book club discussion might reveal that two of the students are only rarely making connections between their comments and those of their peers. The teacher may then provide some specific instruction on using a graphic organizer to capture the group's ideas. An example of a checklist for use during a book club discussion can be seen in figure 2.3.

Figure 2.3   Book Club Checklist

Name of Student: _____ Date: _____

Discussion Text: _____

Book Club Discussion Behaviors	Not in Evidence	Emerging	In Use
PREPARATION Has read selection prior to group discussion			
Has written in response journal			
Has noted unfamiliar words or phrases			
GROUP BEHAVIORS Asks other group members questions about the text			
Extends other students' responses			
Respects the opinions of others			
CONNECTIONS Makes connections between text and self			
Makes connections between focus text and other readings			
Makes connections between text and other students' responses			
OTHER NOTES			

Rubrics

Rubrics are most often used in the assessment of writing, but are useful in other disciplines as well (Custer, 1995; Flood, Lapp, & Wood, 1997). For example, Leitze and Mau (1999) used a rubric to assess problem-solving activities in math. Huffman (1998) used a rubric to assess student learning in art production and noted that the rubric provided students with a visual guide as they completed their assignments. Finally, Carr (1997) used a rubric to assess his students' ability to utilize current multimedia resources to combine sounds and images and produce a soundtrack for their lives.

By using rubrics, students are likely to understand the important elements for which they will be graded. Rubrics differentiate good from poor papers by providing students with criteria for each grade (Spandel & Stiggins, 1997). They also relieve the teacher of having to use subjective criteria for grading. While the development of the rubric is critical, teaching students how to use a rubric and understand the criteria of the rubric is even more important. Research suggests that when writing assessments only focus on mechanics, students' writing skills are not developed (Dahl & Farnan, 1998). Research also suggests that students should be involved in establishing the criteria for the rubric and, by doing so more clearly understand the task at hand and can focus their performance toward the expected outcome. Figure 2.4 provides an example of a writing rubric. However, we know that teachers will use this as a starting point and develop rubrics of their own in partnership with students.

Portfolio Assessments

Performance samples like portfolios refer to some form of student work that remains as an artifact for reflection by teachers, students, and parents. The original use of the term portfolio came from the collections of best works maintained by artists and architects. In education, portfolios more typically consist of samples that represent particular genres of tasks over a period of time rather than students' best work (Hiebert & Frey in press). Even so, the idea of examining samples of work that come from everyday settings, rather than from test settings, is restructuring assessment in many classrooms (Calfee & Gearhart, 1998).

As with all assessment, portfolios require clearly defined goals and purposes, data collection that traverses time and task, and a system of interpretation (Calfee & Hiebert, 1991). A confusion of purpose can lead to the creation of portfolios that simply serve as collection bins of random student work (Wilcox, 1997). One way to establish clear purpose is to develop the expectations for the portfolio with students. In this manner, both student and teacher can brainstorm criteria for selection of pieces to go into the portfolio, as well as identify types of pieces that serve as evidence of mastery. This "portfolio pedagogy" (Yancey, 1992) can guarantee meaningful effort for both student and teacher.

Although the purposes of the portfolio shape its organizational structure, some elements are advisable for any portfolio. Winograd and Arrington (1999) suggest the following:

- A table of contents
- Samples of daily work
- Drafts and revisions of written work

Figure 2.4　Sample Writing Rubric

	Distinguished	Prominent	Proficient	Not Proficient
Thesis	Clearly defined, sustained throughout Topic effectively limited	Thesis defined Topic limited, but noted exceptions	Stated Attempt to limit topic	Unclear or unidentifiable No attempt to limit topic
Development	Topic thoroughly developed throughout with specific examples to support thesis	Topic developed with reasonable evidence	Topic developed General supporting evidence	Topic not clearly developed Unnecessary information
Organization	Highly organized plan with effective transitions Superior introduction and conclusion clearly relate to whole	Organized plan, but weak transitions Introduction or conclusion relate to the whole	Logical organization, with inconsistent transitions Introduction and conclusion do not clearly relate to whole	No organizational plan No attempt to create unity No transitions
Research	Ten or more qualified sources cited appropriately	Ten or more sources but not cited appropriately	Fewer than ten qualified sources cited	Fewer than ten sources cited
Mechanics (e.g., punctuation, spelling, grammar)	Superior editing Fewer than five total errors in paper	Good editing Fewer that one error per page	Careful editing Fewer than two errors per page	Careless editing More than two errors per page

- Student self-evaluations
- Goals written by the student, teacher, and family
- Student-teacher conference records
- Other observational information collected by the teacher

Portfolios are a powerful example of the recursive nature of assessment and instruction. When used well, they not only aid in the teaching of new skills, but also support the continued polishing of students' habits of mind through guided reflection.

Conferencing

The act of conferencing with a student in a one-on-one setting can have a considerable effect on both participants, because the opportunities for such interactions are all too rare in busy classrooms. Conferences may be informal and relatively short (just a few minutes), or longer, with a structured script of questions to engage the learner. Either way, the goal of conferencing with a student is to promote the student's own ability to assess and reflect (Winograd & Arrington, 1999).

Much of the practice for this kind of classroom interaction comes from what we know about supporting student writers (Calkins, 1986; Graves, 1983). In writing workshops, conferences are scheduled throughout the student's evolving work, creating multiple opportunities for the student to interact with the teacher (Dahl & Farnan, 1998). Teachers in responsive curriculum classrooms report that they need opportunities to talk in-depth with individual students about specific topics or tasks, and the use of a structured conference form assists them in engaging in meaningful talk. An example of a conferencing form appears in figure 2.5.

Time is a teacher's most precious commodity, and finding opportunities to conference with students can be a challenge. Even so, setting time aside to talk with individuals can provide information teachers might not gain otherwise. While the task of meeting individually with 30 or 35 students may seem daunting, teachers in responsive curriculum classrooms set daily goals of conferencing with only one or two students. This can be achieved during sustained silent reading or during center rotations. By meeting daily with a small number of students, the teacher can conference with each member of the class over the course of a few weeks. Wise practitioners recognize that the investment of a bit of time to conference with a student promotes student self-reflection (Paris & Ayres, 1994).

Peer Reviews

Teachers in responsive curriculum classrooms seek to move away from the outdated model of a teacher-centered classroom, and toward student-centered learning and teaching. A promising practice in student-centered learning lies in the use of the peer reviews that are part of meaningful writing experiences (Atwell, 1998; Calkins, 1986). The goal of peer reviews is to involve students in the evaluation process and to build their evaluative and interactive skills (Flood, Lapp, & Wood, 1997). There are two commonly used forms of peer review. One is the peer conference, where a small group of students meets to discuss a work in progress. The other is in a large group setting, with a student sitting in the au-

Figure 2.5   Conferencing Form

Name of Student: _____ Date: _____

Description of student work used in this conference: _____

_____

_____

QUESTIONS ABOUT PERFORMANCE

What do you like about this piece?

What would you change?

QUESTIONS ABOUT PROCESS

What was the best strategy you used to complete this piece?

What did you do when you had a problem with this piece?

QUESTIONS ABOUT PERCEPTION

What makes you a good reader? A good writer?

What goals do you have for yourself this year?

Have you achieved the goals you have set for yourself?

What help do you need to reach your goals?

Figure 2.6   Peer Conference Sandwich

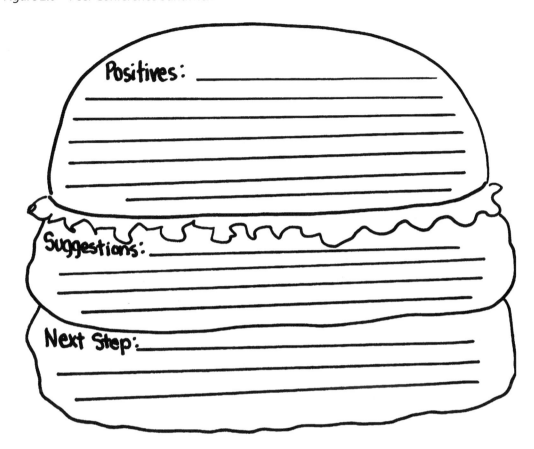

thor's chair to share a piece (Cunningham, Hall, & Defee, 1998). The "author's chair" provides an opportunity for a student to publicly read a finished work, while the peer conference provides a forum for a student writer to interact more intently with classmates while focusing on a composition in a formative stage. The reports of many teachers suggest that children become more knowledgeable about their command of writing as a result of such experiences (e.g., Freedman, 1995; Lobach, 1995).

The success of peer involvement in writing suggests that such interactions hold promise for students' involvement in monitoring, planning, and assessing their comprehension. However, as with all classroom processes, the skills required to effectively collaborate with peers must be explicitly taught and monitored so that equity and communication difficulties can be circumvented (Henkin, 1995). A simple frame for student use in giving constructive feedback is the "sandwich." In this model, students use three stages of conversation: The first layer consists of praise for the piece, with specific positive examples. Constructive criticism forms the "meat" of the discussion, with suggestions for improvement. Finally, the peer conference finishes with an identified next step for the writer. An example of a peer conference worksheet appears in figure 2.6. The use of a peer conference form allows the teacher to monitor the quality of the peer conference while providing another form of assessment information.

Self-Assessment

In many classrooms, the primary evaluator is the teacher. On those infrequent occasions when students participate in the assessment process, their involvement is nominal, such as checking a fellow student's work against the answers the teacher has written on the board. Far rarer is the classroom where children are asked to identify goals and monitor their progress toward those goals. The consequences of an exclusive reliance on externally driven assessment systems can have a negative effect on student achievement and attitude toward learning (Ames & Ames, 1984; Johnston & Winograd, 1985; Paris & Winograd, 1989). The use of self-assessment can serve as a motivator for students, as well as support their learning (Perry, 1998).

Several promising developments suggest greater student involvement in planning and monitoring learning. The emphasis of the last decade on brain-based learning is an example of such a development. Neurobiologists have shown that the search for meaning is innate, and that meaning emanates from the learner, not the teacher (Diamond & Hopson, 1998). Employment of self-assessment opportunities in daily practice increases each learner's ability to seek and identify goals that are personally meaningful.

Guides that assist students in self-assessment or in peer assessment are a feature in many literacy books and journals (e.g., Courtney & Abodeeb, 1999; Lapp, Fisher, Flood, & Cabello, 2000). Although such guides are popular in writing instruction, especially for editing and revising, some instruments are also oriented to aiding students in assessing their ability to plan and monitor their reading (e.g., Allen & Gonzalez, 1998). The self-evaluation guide in figure 2.7 is for self-assessment over the course of a culminating project. Students plan and reflect at the beginning, middle, and end of the project. This self-assessment then becomes part of the project itself. Students who are taught to plan and monitor their work habits begin to take ownership in their work.

Another example of guiding students in self-assessment comes from Project Zero (Chen, Krechevsky, Isberg, & Viens, 1998; Wolf, 1989), which uses portfolios for assessment of writing and fine arts. While teachers interact with students in deciding what to put into portfolios, students are responsible for their selections. Furthermore, portfolios include a diary or journal in which students reflect on the progress they detect in their portfolio entries.

Assessing one's abilities and gauging the next step is an important part of any type of learning. This element has received increased attention in literacy programs (Bauer, 1999), and indications are that emphases on metacognition and writing processes are creating more opportunities for students to assess their progress (Burchell & Westmoreland, 1999).

Assessments in the Classroom

Ms. Kelly used a variety of assessments with her fifth graders. For example, she used an end-of-unit map test that she created to assess content knowledge, a writing rubric that the class developed to assess student writing, a peer evaluation worksheet to assess cooperative groups, a skills checklist to assess vocabulary development, and a KWL chart to assess information gained throughout the unit.

Figure 2.7   Self-Assessment Form

SELF-ASSESSMENT OF PROJECT PERFORMANCE

Name: _____   Project: _____

_____

Before Project   ***Date:*** _____

My goal(s) for this project:

Steps I need to take in order to meet my goal(s):

_____

Mid-Project   ***Date:*** _____

Am I on target for meeting my goal(s)?

What do I need to do in order to meet my target?

_____

Project Completion   ***Date:*** _____

Did I achieve my goal(s)?

Why or Why not?

What are the strategies that worked for me?

What will I do differently next time?

Similarly, Ms. Scott used a KWL as part of her pre-assessment of student knowledge about explorers, a writing rubric to assess their journal reflections, a checklist to assess their Cornell note-taking skills, and a one-to-one conference to assess their understanding of archaeology.

Ms. Gutierrez used a number of assessments in her unit. During the literature circles, she used a Book Club Checklist. She also used a checklist to assess her students' ability to conduct Internet searches. She used a KWL chart to understand her students' knowledge of Vietnam and immigration. Further, she used a writing rubric to assess their character analysis papers and their literature circle journal entries. Finally, she required that students regularly self-assess their performance and behavior in her classroom.

Ongoing assessment is also an important way to monitor student progress. These formative assessments allow the teacher to determine if all students are assuming more control of the content as instruction progresses. A student who is not making sufficient progress can be retaught, using a classroom peer tutor, or in a teacher-directed small group with others who can benefit from a review of the material.

Chapter 3

IDENTIFY RICHLY DETAILED SOURCE MATERIAL

The use of richly detailed source material that represents a variety of student learning styles and intelligences assures that each student in the class has access to the knowledge base in the topic being studied (Onosko & Jorgensen, 1997). Too often, teachers put students with reading difficulties at a distinct disadvantage from the start by failing to augment print-based information sources. Textbooks used in content instruction can be limiting when they are used to the exclusion of other materials. For example, most students would better understand a lecture on DNA if the teacher included an activity wherein the students take apart and put together a three-dimensional model of the complex double-helix molecule. Thus, this chapter provides a discussion about selecting materials that are appropriate and responsive to the needs of students and how to use the textbook and other richly detailed sources.

Using Textbooks Effectively

Using content standards requires teachers to continue to emphasize the textbook as a primary source (Massich & Munoz, 1996) while developing lessons in which students can experience learning through hands-on activities (Christ, 1995). Relying on the text is not unfamiliar to teachers (Squire, 1987). However, doing so and also meeting all of these additional challenges is often overwhelming. During social studies instruction, teachers usually rely even more heavily on books to create images of the past (Moss, 1991) and to explore the majority of social studies issues. In fact, several studies have shown that, in elementary schools, the textbook composes as much as 90% of the instructional time in social studies (Shaver, Davis, & Helburn, 1980; Woodward, Elliott, & Nagel, 1986). But the textbook cannot do the whole job alone. Many other sources are needed to supplement the textbook. The types of books and materials selected by teachers for social studies units have received increased attention over the past decade (Lapp, Flood, & Farnan, 1996; Ross, 1997).

Consider the perspective offered by a textbook: It serves as a summary of the *textbook authors'* knowledge of the content. While valuable, it is several degrees removed from the primary-source information used by the authors in developing the textbook. When all the events and historical figures of World War II may occupy a few pages in the World History textbook, there is little room for the details. Since textbooks can only rarely provide a comprehensive picture of the period of study, instruction often becomes focused on memorizing the facts and chronology of events. History textbooks, while presenting correct factual information (Romanowski, 1996), often provide a narrow, singular perspective (Banks, 1973; Tunnell & Ammon, 1996). With widespread attention being given to the integration of literacy across the curriculum during the past ten years, many teachers who use the textbook as a resource also supplement it with literature selections (Combs & Beach, 1994; Johnson & Ebert, 1992; Moss, 1991).

The difficulty of the textbooks is also problematic for many readers. The textbooks themselves are written at an assigned grade level, and the readability of the text excludes many students from access to the material held in its chapters. The gold standard for reading is the ability to comprehend—to make meaning of the words on the page. But when text is at a frustration level for some students (typically defined as reading 89% or less of the words correctly), comprehension is compromised. Without other supporting materials, these students slip further behind their classmates in content knowledge.

The range of student reading levels in secondary classrooms requires teachers to plan curriculum in a different fashion. Wise practitioners plan for a span of four grade levels (two below grade level, at grade level, and one above grade level) in order to increase access to the content. This is not as difficult as it may appear, because teachers using responsive curriculum design recognize that the textbook is merely one source, and not the definer of the curriculum itself. Using a unit organized around a central question, a teacher can then assemble a wide range of materials in many mediums and at many readability levels. In a tenth grade World History class, the teacher knew the students would better understand a lecture on World War II and the Holocaust if the source materials included the textbook, a videotape of a survivor, actual letters written during the time in *Anne Frank: The Diary of a Young Girl* (Frank & Mooyaart, 1993), and personal interviews with their family members who lived during the war. Through the use of multiple mediums, the teacher created source materials at differing reading levels without compromising the integrity of the information. This teacher recognized that the teaching of history is the teaching of stories, and that the complexities of people's lives are best represented in the histories of individuals. The use of these richly detailed source materials also better equips the students to answer the central question, "How does war affect those who do not fight?"

Intermediality

The world has been profoundly effected by the explosion of available information. For instance, technology has shortened the production time necessary to write books. Twenty years ago, there were approximately 5,000 children's books in print; in 1999, that figure had reached 89,000. Delivery of information has also rapidly expanded into mediums that did not yet exist even a decade ago. The Internet has become a major force in the dissemination of information, few businesses today are without a website, and customers increasingly expect the Internet to be the point of sale.

The expansion of information sources creates new demands on today's learner. Viewing is now recognized as a dimension of literacy, along with speaking, listening, reading, and writing (Flood & Lapp, 1995). Increased reliance on media and technology has led to new understandings of literacy and learning (Lapp, Flood, & Fisher, 1999; Semali & Pailliotet, 1999). Flood and Lapp (1995) propose a "broader conceptualization in which literacy is defined as the ability to function competently in the 'communicative arts,' which include the language arts as well as the visual arts of drama, art, film, video, and television" (p. 1). These new forms of visual and information literacy are changing the very nature of schooling (Dahl & Farnan, 1998; Messaris, 1994). For example, one new area of inquiry focuses on accessing information through multiple forms of media—intermediality. While a consensus definition of intermediality has yet to emerge, generally speaking, it involves multiple forms of both text and media, including books, videos, life experiences, websites, films, posters, CD-ROMs, illustrations, and the like. Advances in technology significantly influence these multiple forms of media. Technology permeates our world—cellular phones, computers, fax machines, VCRs, just to name a few. Students in our schools must not only learn to read, but they must also learn to access information for a variety of purposes.

Recent research indicates that using multiple sources of information increases comprehension, critical thinking, and recall (Lapp, Flood, & Fisher, 1999; Koretz, 1999). Frey (1998) reported increased levels of understanding and more frequent responses at the aesthetic level when her fourth graders had access to multiple information sources. Similarly, Massich and Munoz (1996) described the success they experienced with their middle school students, especially English language learners, as they taught a civil war unit with multiple information sources, including visuals, realia, music, documents, and diaries. Evans (1997) suggests that social studies instruction should be based on inquiry, problem solving, and critical thinking. It seems that if this type of instruction were to become a reality, the use of multiple and varied sources would motivate students to become active thinkers who are challenged by alternative viewpoints.

Types of Source Materials

Children's and Young Adult Literature

Historical and realistic fiction written for young readers serves as a boon for teachers in responsive curriculum classrooms. The use of trade books not only infuses well-written literature into the curriculum, it also provides multiple perspectives at varied levels of text difficulty. The availability of literature for use in content areas has expanded rapidly in the last decade. By example, in addressing the range of reading levels in a history classroom studying the role of children in the Middle Ages, a teacher offers several different pieces of literature. Using the criteria of well-written fiction featuring a child protagonist in a medieval setting, students can read either *Catherine, Called Birdy* (Cushman, 1995), *Adam of the Road* (1987), or *Otto of the Silver Hand* (Pyle, 1967). While the three books reflect a wide range of readability, all are united in setting and theme. The large group discussions led by the teacher lead to the creation of a graphic organizer synthesizing each book's main characters, the problems they face, and the solutions to those challenges. These student responses are then compared to the information presented in the textbook, assisting students in connecting the protagonists' stories to historical events.

Poetry

The power of poetry as a richly detailed source material lies in its economy of words. Well-chosen poetry selections can convey content knowledge, as well as carry an emotional message. The accessibility of poetry can encourage reluctant readers. For instance, science text on insects can be augmented with the fourteen bug poems of *Joyful Noise: Poems for Two Voices* (Fleischman, 1988). Paralleling a study of the migration of workers from Mexico, the experiences of Mexican-American children in the Southwestern United States are represented in *Canto Familiar* (Soto, 1996). Weather and seasons are beautifully portrayed in the Japanese haiku poetry of Issa and Basho, in such collections as *Cool Melons-Turn to Frogs! The Life and Poems of Issa* (Gollub, 1998) and *Grass Sandals: The Travels of Basho* (Spivak, 1997). Even complex geometry and algebra concepts can be portrayed through the use of the poems in *Math Talk: Mathematical Ideas in Poems for Two Voices* (Pappas, 1991). Other collections by notable poets contain myriad subject matter. These include the works of Jack Prelutsky (1996) in *Pizza the Size of the Sun* and Carl Sandburg (1995) in *Poetry for Young People*.

Biographies and Autobiographies

Biographies of historical figures offer the richness of human experience, set in the context of notable events in history. Many biographies of children and adults facing extraordinary circumstances exist in popular literature. Biographies can also be used to explore an entire genre of experience. A study of notable book authors gives students an opportunity to connect popular works with a writer's experiences. A unit of instruction could examine the lives of Jerry Spinelli (1998) in *Knots in My Yo-Yo String: The Autobiography of a Kid* and Gary Paulsen (1999) in *My Life in Dog Years*. The experiences of Japanese citizens and Japanese American citizens during World War II are examined in the books *Shin's Tricycle* (Kodama, 1995), *Sadako and the Thousand Paper Cranes* (Coerr, 1999), and *The Invisible Thread: An Autobiography* (Uchida, 1995). And of course, biographies can also be used to focus on a remarkable life. Examples include *Girl of the Shining Mountains: Sacagawea's Story* (Roop, 1999), *The Amazing Life of Benjamin Franklin* (Giblin, 2000), *Escape from Slavery: The Boyhood of Frederick Douglass in His Own Words* (Douglass, 1994), *Meet the Great Composers* (Montgomery & Hinson, 1995), *Lives of the Musicians: Good Times, Bad Times (and What the Neighbors Thought)* (Krull, 1993), and *Sebastian: A Book About Bach* (Winter, 1999). Biographies present a fascinating window on the lives of the famous, the infamous, and those thrust into extraordinary circumstances.

Picture Books

Picture books? Yes, picture books can provide older students an interesting look at a topic of study (Goerss, 1998). Picture books also reinforce vocabulary, language skills such as word rhyming, and story sequence. Picture books have been successfully used in middle school classrooms to encourage reluctant readers to participate in content area instruction (Cassady, 1998). Miller (1998) believes that picture books build connections to learning experiences for early adolescents in all content areas.

Picture books have been used as a supplement to the textbook in many upper grade and secondary school classrooms across the country. For example, Beck, Gilles, O'Connor, and Koblitz (1999), provide a list of 33 books, including picture books, that give children insight into living in the great Midwest and into westward expansion. Mundy and Hadaway (1999) used picture books about weather to provide supplemental instruction for high school ESL students. Matanzo and Richardson (1998) describe how the picture book rendition of the operatic story "Aida" was used with secondary school students to introduce operas.

Awards such as the Newbery and the Caldecott Medals are given yearly and also provide educators with information about new books. The Newbery Award is based on literary quality, the Caldecott on the quality of the illustrations. The medal and honor winners are selected by committees that read all of the books published during the year.

The Coretta Scott King Award is presented annually to both an African-American author and an African-American illustrator for outstanding contributions to children's literature. Organizations such as the International Reading Association (IRA) and the National Council of Teachers of English (NCTE) have established committees that annually develop lists of notable books. IRA's Teacher's Choices is a national project involving teachers in the selection of books for use across the curriculum. The Teacher's Choices lists are published annually in *The Reading Teacher*.

Diaries and Letters

Students often view the lives and events of the past as disconnected and irrelevant to their lives. History through this lens becomes simply a task of memorizing dates and names for later use on a test. The use of ephemera (papers that reflect an historical era or event) in classrooms can breathe life into historical topics. While actual items are not available outside museums, many letters, journals, and diaries have been reproduced for student use. Probably the most famous is the Anne Frank diary, and others are available as well. An outstanding example is *We Are Witnesses: Five Diaries of Teenagers Who Died in the Holocaust* (Boas, 1996). Besides telling the story of Anne Frank, four other teens relate their experiences, serving as a chilling reminder of just how many lives were taken in the Holocaust. *Zlata's Diary: A Child's Life in Sarajevo* (Filipovic, 1995) is the journal of an eleven-year-old child in war-torn Bosnia. A teacher can first present the factual information about an important event, then contrast it with an entry from a diary. *Anastasia's Album* (Tanaka, 1996) is designed like a scrapbook, and tells the story of Anastasia, youngest daughter of the last czar of Russia. Photographs, drawings, letters, and other memorabilia reflect Anastasia's life up until her death at the hands of revolutionaries at the age of eleven. Younger students can learn about the life of Benjamin Banneker, a noted African-American astronomer and almanac author, in *Dear Benjamin Banneker* (Pinkney, 1998). Excerpts of letters between Banneker and Thomas Jefferson are used to tell the story of these two remarkable Americans. The diaries and letters used in class can be extended by having students write original journal entries about the lives they are studying. This use of simulation in writing can increase a student's understanding of the concepts being taught (Schneider & Jackson, 2000).

Music

Music is a powerful way to motivate students to read (Towell, 1999). Not only do students read the song texts, but they often become interested in a topic of study and search out books related to the songs they like. For example, Alvermann and Hagood (2000) found that focusing on students' music interest led to increased interest in school literacy practices. The challenge for teachers is to find appropriate music for the content they teach. Probably the easiest way to do this is to collaborate with the music educator at the school site. In addition, several websites related to children's music exist (http://www.childrensmusic.org/).

Some examples of the use of music in content area instruction include the song *Follow the Drinking Gourd* as the introduction to a unit of study on slavery. A ninth grade English teacher used the song *Isn't It Ironic* to focus on irony in novels. A tenth grade earth science teacher collected a number of songs, including *Oh, Watch the Stars, Haley Came to Jackso*n, and *Star Light, Star Bright* to remind students about the cultural interest in the night sky.

Websites

The emergence of the Internet as a source for material to use in classrooms has challenged many teachers. After all, most teachers' experience in school did not include Internet resources. Additionally, there are many warnings about students accessing inappropriate websites that feature violence, pornography, and hate speech. The combination of being unsure of how to use Internet resources in the classroom and concern about the content of websites has made some educators reluctant to use these source materials. However, students need to be competent at locating web sources and analyzing the worthiness of the content. Judicious use of Internet resources can teach students both of these important skills.

The first step in using websites as source material is determining whether it serves a purpose. Internet sources should not be used simply to fulfill a technology requirement, but rather should be utilized when they offer information that expands students' understanding of the concepts being taught. When exploring potential Internet websites for use in the classroom, ask these questions:

1. Does this site contain information that is accurate?
2. Would the site be easy to use by students?
3. Does it identify the hosting institution?
4. When was it last updated?
5. Are there links to other sites? Are those links of similar quality?

When suitable websites have been identified, the next step is to construct opportunities for students to use them. Many teachers introduce websites to their students by creating a learning station for use in center rotations. The teacher bookmarks the websites in advance, then creates a task for students to complete. A simple introductory lesson for a new website is a scavenger hunt. An excellent site is http://www.nationalgeographic.com/kids. A scavenger hunt for this site could target regular features of the site, including its geography bee, pen pals network, and amazing facts. This allows students to practice scrolling and navigating around the site while creating a challenge for them to complete. As students become more comfortable with the mechanics of a website, more can be introduced, this time with the task being to use the content the site offers. In a unit about planets, a teacher bookmarked the National Geographic site; http://www.discovery.com, sponsored by the Discovery Channel; and http://kids.msfc.nasa.gov, the NASA website designed for students. Students used these three websites for information about their group's planet, along with more conventional sources. Other outstanding websites that serve as excellent reference materials include http://www.louvre.fr, which provides an online tour of the Louvre's collection, and http://www.whitehouse.gov/WH/kids/html/home.html, for information about the President and the United States government.

The ultimate goal for students is to be able to evaluate websites themselves, so that they can critically analyze information. Like other forms of information, Internet websites represent wide variability in terms of quality, accuracy, and design. This means that students require explicit instruction on how to view Internet information, being taught to ask questions, much like those a teacher asks when examining a potential website. This may be done in the form of a rubric. An example of a rubric for student use appears in figure 3.1.

Guest Speakers

Collaboration between schools and community members is not a new idea. However, at the secondary level, many school personnel do not know how to effectively use community members as part of the curriculum. Guest speakers are one way that professionals or community members with unique experiences or lives can be invited into the school system (Wortmann, 1992). Guest speakers allow students to talk with a variety of people about historical events, career options, new developments in technology, life experiences, and so on (Pokrywcaynski, 1992).

Finding good guest speakers can be a trial-and-error process. Potential guest speakers must be invited, listened to, and evaluated by the teachers and students. At least three important considerations for guest speakers must be considered. First, the speaker's style is important. Does this person have the presentation skills necessary to engage young adults? Second, the speaker's qualifications are important. Does this person have the background to answer questions that students will have? Finally, the content of the speech is important. Does this person understand the age-appropriate nature of the content? Does this person understand the curriculum of the class and how his or her speech will support the overall curriculum? Sometimes guest speakers need to be reminded to bring audio-visual materials with them—especially if they have artifacts from the field or historical events.

Figure 3.1   Student Rubric for Evaluating Internet Websites

Website Address: _____

Name of Hosting Institution: _____

	Outstanding	Adequate	No Evidence
EASE OF USE			
Easy to load			
Clear site map available			
Help available			
DESIGN			
Links to other sites work			
Good use of graphics			
Text fits on one page			
CONTENT			
Accuracy of information			
Completeness of information			
Linked sites are of similar quality			
CREDIBILITY			
Contact information available			
Host institution named			
Site is regularly updated			

To ensure that students attend to the guest speaker, teachers often require students to take notes during the presentation and to submit those notes for review by the teacher (Van Nordstrand, 1998). In addition, many teachers spend the class session prior to the guest speaker identifying questions in advance so that the audience can participate in a meaningful conversation with the guest speaker. Teachers have found that identifying questions in advance also provides some anticipation and interest in the guest speaker's presentation. Finally, many teachers invite students to evaluate guest speakers using a form similar to the one found in figure 3.2.

Figure 3.2   Student Evaluation for Guest Speaker

Speaker: _____

Topic: _____

1. I thought the things the speaker said were interesting.

   Yes   No   Somewhat

2. I understood what the speaker was discussing.

   Yes   No   Somewhat

3. I would like to learn more about this topic or profession.

   Yes   No   Somewhat

4. I know more about this topic or profession than I did before this guest speaker.

   Yes   No   Somewhat

5. This profession interests me as a possible career choice.

   Yes   No   Somewhat   Not Applicable

6. The three most important things that I learned during this presentation are:

7. The questions that I still have include:

_____

Using the Community as a Classroom

Instruction outside of classroom walls provides teachers and students with opportunities to apply what has been learned within a real world context. It reinforces the importance and usefulness of what has been learned previously, while challenging students about new areas to explore. We hesitate to use the words "field trip," because that terminology represents an outdated model of the trip itself as a culminating activity. Rather, we prefer to view the world as a classroom, with trips as an extension of teaching and learning.

In order to maximize the impact of a community visit, students must be prepared for the experience. Community experiences are an ideal opportunity to expand the vocabulary of students, particularly English language learners. However, their initial exposure to the new vocabulary should not be in the community. Vocabulary instruction must first occur in the classroom, so that learners can then refine their understanding through the community experience. Students also benefit from the availability of a graphic organizer to capture their observations. An example of such an organizer is shown in figure 3.3.

Figure 3.3   Community Experience Organizer

Today we are going to _____
_____

The purpose of our trip is _____
_____

Gathering Information

I talked to _____ and I learned
_____
_____
_____

I saw _____ and I learned _____
_____
_____
_____
_____

I did _____ and I learned _____
_____
_____
_____

After the Community Experience:

Things I didn't know before today _____

_____

_____

_____

_____

Connections to things I already knew _____

_____

_____

_____

_____

What I still need to find out about _____

_____

_____

_____

_____

Using Information Sources in Classrooms

Information sources permeate the classrooms of our focus teachers. Each has a well-stocked classroom library with over 400 titles in each classroom, which is often used for independent reading. Thus, in addition to the school library, students in these classrooms can access poetry, children's literature, biographies, and picture books at any time. Beyond the classrooms libraries, these three teachers incorporate additional information sources based on their unit of study.

In Ms. Kelly's unit on explorers, she invited students to use a computer program about explorers, the social studies text, maps of the world, and a compass. She read aloud several books to her class, including *Explorers* (Fradin, 1984), *Six Brave Explorers: A Pop-Up Book* (Moerbeek & Dijs, 1997), and *Follow the Dream* (Sis, 1996). The students also visited the local space exploration museum during one class day.

In Ms. Scott's unit on archaeologists, she invited students to search the World Wide Web for information on archaeology, read their social studies tesxt *Across the Centuries*, view a video on the discovery of the pyramids, listen to her read aloud the newspaper article on the discovery of King Tut's tomb and the picture book *Discovery* (Brodsky, 1999), and participate in a shared reading of *Right Here on This Spot* (Addy, 1999). Students also listened to music appropriate to the various parts of the world they studied such as African drums, Egyptian chants, and Asian melodies, and were engaged with a guest lecturer who was an archaeologists from the local university.

Ms. Gutierrez used the novel *Goodbye, Vietnam* (Whelan, 19993) as the core book for her unit. She began her unit of study with a read aloud of the picture book *Who Belongs Here? An American Story* (Knight, 1993). In addition, she invited students to view websites about Vietnam, view a video about a dramatic rescue of a refugee boat in Indonesian waters, keep diaries as if they were forced to leave their homes, read the diaries and other personal narratives from the book *Voices from Vietnam* (Denenberg, 1997), learn at least one poem from the book *An Anthology of Vietnamese Poems: From the Eleventh Through the Twentieth Centuries* (Huynh, 1996), and discuss immigration experiences with an adult who was a recent arrival from Vietnam. She also added a number of children's picture books about Vietnam to her classroom library, including: *Journey Home* (McKay, 1998), *The Lotus Seed* (Garland, 1997), and *The Crystal Heart: A Vietnamese Legend* (Shepard, 1998).

Chapter 4

DESIGNING INTERRELATED DAILY LESSONS AND CULMINATING ACTIVITIES

All students need to have explicit connections made among individual daily learning experiences. Teachers must assure that daily activities logically build students' knowledge throughout the unit to enable them to use the newly acquired body of knowledge to answer the overarching unit question. For example, these three activities might accomplish this goal: identifying various viewpoints or positions regarding the unit's central issue or problem; identifying key concepts, events, or persons related to the issue under consideration; and identifying and answering questions that need to be considered to intelligently address the problem or issue.

For example, while reading *Of Mice and Men* (Steinbeck, 1937), students created character webs and concept maps based on the book. Character webs are updated after each chapter—students illustrate characters as they meet them and write phrases that describe the individual (with page number references) around the illustration. Concept or semantic maps are spatial representations of the main points of the chapter completed in groups of four students (for more information, see Lapp, Flood, & Hoffman, 1996). Reviewing the character webs and concept maps allows the teachers to assess their students' comprehension. Additional assessments, such as quick writes, found poems, and impromptu speeches, allow teachers to gauge the learning of everyone in the class. Thus, this chapter focuses on instructional design and culminating projects.

Instructional Design

Stephen Covey, an organizational management and leadership mentor, advises to begin with the end in mind (Covey, 1990). His words are just as true when discussing lesson planning. Experienced teachers know the value of planning to ensure that learning occurs for all students. And key to effective planning is the ability to articulate what the student outcomes will be and how they will be evidenced. Questions to ask when planning a lesson include the following:

- What are the key concepts?
- What should students do with these concepts?

- What activities will provide students with the opportunity to practice these concepts?
- How much time is available?
- What assessment methods will be used to determine students' mastery?

Teachers in responsive curriculum classrooms also acknowledge the social nature of teaching and learning (Green, Harker, & Golden, 1987). The most carefully crafted lesson can fail dismally if the teacher does not recognize the reciprocal relationship between instructor and learners in revising and reshaping the lesson in progress. As students gain (or fail to gain) understanding of the lesson, the demands of the lesson may shift, necessitating the reteaching or extension of the original concepts. In effective lessons, careful planning is coupled with attention to the interactions of students, to continually reconstruct the lesson (Doyle, 1996).

Many models of lesson plan frames exist, (e.g., Hunter, 1994; Macdonald & Purpel, 1987; Slavin, 1995) but nearly all contain similar elements. The use of a frame for lesson planning can serve as a reminder to teachers to consider many of the variables that can influence the success of the lesson. The steps of the lessons can be best crafted through the use of a series of statements. Let's look at seven components of a dynamic lesson (see figure 4.1).

"This is our purpose": Learning objectives and standards

The first step in lesson planning is to determine the purpose for the lesson. The purpose for a lesson should not be an isolated skill unconnected to other learning, put rather should state in observable and measurable terms exactly what a student will be able to do and how they will demonstrate mastery. These learning objectives are best stated through the use of action verbs like "classify" or "estimate," rather than vague and difficult-to-measure constructs like "understand" or "know." These learning objectives are then used to determine assessment measures of student success. In addition, many schools now require the use of content area standards in lesson planning to ensure that student experiences match the learning goals of the district and state. Content standards are usually broader than learning objectives, and are often written to encompass instruction that spans an entire grade level. The learning objectives cited in the lesson should advance students toward mastery of the standards. As noted in chapter 1, social and communication objectives for the lesson should be also be considered. Teachers in responsive classrooms know that addressing only content or academic objectives does not facilitate the development of the whole student.

"Here's what we're doing today": Anticipatory set

In order to enhance the learning of students, begin the lesson with a short activity or prompt that will focus their attention. This anticipatory set alerts them to the topic or concept being studied, preparing them for the lesson. These activities are brief in nature (one to five minutes), and can include an advance organizer (Ausubel, 1978) to brief students on the day's events. Other examples of anticipatory set activities include posting a question related to the day's lesson on the board or reading a story that will prompt discussion and response.

Figure 4.1   Sample Lesson Plan Format

Subject: _____   Grade Level: _____

Date: _____   Duration: _____

Learning Objectives:

Content Standards:

Anticipatory Set:

Instruction:

Guided Practice:

Independent Practice:

Assessment and Closure:

Reflection:

"Let me show you": Instruction and modeling

This phase is the most closely associated with traditional teaching. During instruction, content is explicitly presented to students, and the teacher's level of control is high. Connections between prior knowledge and the new concepts or skills are also taught through the use of graphic organizers, semantic maps, and other strategies. Modeling is interwoven into instruction, and students are shown in a graphic form or through demonstration what the finished product looks like. While instruction and modeling are essential components of a lesson, they are not the end goal. Rather, the purpose is to move students to guided practice, the true heart of a lesson.

"Follow me": Guided practice

The centerpiece of an effective lesson is the progress students achieve when receiving some support. This practice echoes Lev Vygotsky's (1978) theory of "zones of proximal development." Vygotsky theorized that when children receive support just beyond what they can accomplish independently, they learn new skills and concepts. He defined the zone as

> the distance between the actual developmental level as determined by independent problem solving and the level of potential development as determined through problem solving under adult guidance or in collaboration with more capable peers. (1978, p. 86)

In guided practice, the teacher leads students through the steps necessary to accomplish the goals of the lesson. This learner experiences the support through a pattern of "see, hear, do." By using the combination of visual, auditory, and kinesthetic support, the learner is able to respond at increasingly higher levels of independence. This continuum provides a sliding scale of support for diverse learners, because students who need more or less support can progress at their own pace. This phase should not be rushed, as it serves as the keystone to the lesson.

"Now you try it": Independent practice

At this stage of the lesson, teacher control is further reduced as the learners assume more responsibility. Working independently, or in pairs or small groups, students now practice on their own, applying what they have just been taught. The teacher may circulate and assist, in some cases reteaching in order to clarify understanding.

"What you've learned": Assessment and closure

The end of the lesson is assessment and closure. The purpose of assessment in lesson planning is to gather evidence to determine whether each child has learned what was taught. The learning objectives first outlined at the beginning of the lesson planning process are again used to design the assessment of the lesson. If the learning objective is to graph variables on an x and y axis, then the assessment is whether the students performed the operation correctly. An objective for students to determine major causes for the United States' entry into World War II dictates that the assessment measure products that indicate their ability to articulate reasonable hypotheses about this topic. In all cases, the learning objectives and assessments are tightly related. The use of clearly defined assessment methods in lessons provides to the teacher important information about whether the concepts need to be retaught to individuals, small groups, or the entire class.

Closure signals the students that the lesson is finished. Like an anticipatory set, closure assists students in making connections between prior knowledge and new knowledge. Closure activities are also short in duration, relative to the length of the lesson, and usually consist of a review of the key points of the lesson. An old maxim of teaching still holds true: "Tell them what they'll learn; tell them; then tell them what they learned."

"What did I like? What will I do differently?": Reflection

Another key to teaching and learning is reflective practice. Wise practitioners know that engaging in reflection after the lesson serves to constantly improve teacher effectiveness, because it assists teachers in becoming confident professionals. The role of self-reflection and self-analysis has become a critical element in teacher preparation programs (Freese, 1999) and staff development for in-service teachers (Beerens, 2000).

Reflective practices often analyze student responses and the teacher's own behaviors. Reflection is best done soon after the lesson is over—within 24 hours, if possible. Recall student responses for evidence of understanding. Were many of the questions of a logistical nature? These may indicate that clearer directions are needed. Did student responses incorporate peers' observations? If not, teaching students how to engage in accountable talk may be in order. Review the teacher behaviors as well. Was the time allotted adequate? Did all students have opportunities to respond? If either of these areas are problematic, the teacher can alter subsequent plans.

Culminating Projects

While daily lesson plans have built-in closure activities, they do not signal to students that the unit of study has been completed. Culminating projects are one way that teachers in responsive classrooms meet their goal of gaining closure. Culminating projects are big closure activities that give students opportunities to demonstrate their understanding of the unit's central issue or problem through a product. When teachers provide choices for how students can present their final exhibition, including options for written papers, demonstrations, presentations, and building models, each student has the opportunity to use his or her favored learning style. For example, the students reading *Of Mice and Men* (Steinbeck, 1937) may create a mock trial of George and try him for killing Lenny. Students can be assigned roles such as judge, jury member, lawyers, plaintiff, witnesses, defendant, and print and radio journalists covering the trial. Alternatively, a culminating project focused on the same unit of study could be a visual and written essay focused on "heroes from the Great Depression."

Culminating Classroom Projects

The students in Ms. Kelly's fifth grade class worked in groups and studied explorers. At the end of the unit, each group presented a skit that they had written about the explorer. They used information from their textbook, informational books from the library, videos, and the Internet to piece together the life experiences of their selected explorer. Each group also created a test for the members of their class to take after the presentation. Thus, students in Ms. Kelly's class took five tests on different explorers!

In Ms. Scott's classroom, students presented information to their peers about their archaeological dig. During the presentation, each member of the group discussed the artifacts that they had and the conclusions they reached about their seven artifacts and the people they think the artifacts represent.

In Ms. Gutierrez's ninth grade English class, the students created a human biography of their selected character, which were posted around the classroom for a gallery walk. Half the members of the class stood near their character analysis and talked with peers as they roamed the room. After approximately 30 minutes, students switched. Those who had been standing by their papers walked the room while those who had been walking the room stood near (and explained) their analysis.

Section Two

Instructional Considerations

Chapter 5

LITERACY INSTRUCTION WITH THE CONTENT AREA

We've all heard the maxim: Students beyond grade 3 move from *learning to read* to *reading to learn*. Direct, explicit instruction in decoding is gradually decreased as the content of science, social studies, and mathematics takes on a more prominent role. The amount of text to be read also increases as students progress through the grade levels. The vocabulary requirements continue to grow, as well, as readers encounter the technical terminology and discourse of the hard and soft sciences (Lemke, 1990). A result is that the achievement gap accelerates as readers who struggled in the primary grades fall further behind their peers.

This challenge emerges at precisely the time the role of the teacher is changing, as well. At the secondary level, teachers increasingly identify themselves by their specialty area. Relatively few have formal experience in teaching reading or writing. And the facts are sobering—while the demands of the technology marketplace require graduates with higher proficiency in reading, students continue to lag behind in their acquisition of critical literacy skills (Barton, 1997).

The reading demands of content-area classes can provide ideal opportunities to develop and extend critical literacy skills using informational text (Farnan, 1996). However, many of the teachers of those very same classes also express dismay at exactly how to accomplish this. A recent study of 435 K–12 teachers showed that less than half could identify widely known content-area reading strategies such as KWL (Ogle, 1986), and only 30% actually used it (Spor & Schneider, 1999). Although it is not necessary to transform content-area teachers into reading teachers, it is wise to show them how to infuse defensible literacy strategies into content classes. The remainder of this chapter provides information about the ways in which teachers can infuse literacy instruction into their content. More specifically, this chapter focuses on teaching questioning strategies, discussion strategies to enhance comprehension, textbook feature knowledge, read alouds, vocabulary development, and writing to learn.

Teaching Questioning Strategies

In many traditional classrooms, questioning was controlled by the teacher, who determined when it would begin and end, what topics would be discussed (and what would not), and the extent to which students would participate. These interchanges often followed a predictable recursive sequence called I-R-E or Initiate-Respond-Evaluate (Cazden, 1986; Mehan, 1979). Students in these classrooms came to expect that the teacher would first initiate a question for a student to respond to, then evaluate the answer for accuracy, and finally follow with another question. In this model, the primary responsibility of the student was to furnish a "correct" answer. Rarely were students welcomed to initiate their own questions or to direct their questions to peers. At one time, this model dominated classroom conversation in America's schools. Almasi (1995) reported that the I-R-E sequence comprised 85% of the discussions in her study's fourth grade classrooms! Importantly, the I-R-E pattern of teacher-student interchange rarely allowed for the critical higher-order thinking associated with meaningful learning (Kuhn, 1999). The modeling of these teacher-led questioning patterns furthers the internal questioning students engage in when they read, and values factual knowledge over synthesis and evaluation.

Teachers in responsive curriculum classrooms explicitly teach questioning strategies to foster critical thinking in their students. This encourages students to take an active role in their own learning because they consciously employ these strategies to better comprehend the text and the concepts it is presenting. Two widely taught strategies are Question-Answer Relationship (Raphael, 1986) and Question the Author (Beck, McKeown, Worthy, Sandora, & Kucan, 1993). These techniques support student inquiry into the deeper levels of meaning to be found in narrative and informational text.

Question-Answer Relationship (Raphael, 1986), also known as QAR, is a framework to forward students' understanding of the text-explicit and text-implicit information in their readings (Lapp & Flood, 1992). In the case of "Right There" questions, for example, students refer to one or more locations in the text for the answers. This contrasts with "On My Own" questions that require students to access their background knowledge and experiences. These questions are given to students in advance of a reading to better orient them to the information they should anticipate in the text. It also models what fluent readers already know—that reading is a transaction between both the text and what the reader brings to the text. In addition to identifying types of questions, students are also charged with creating Right There and On My Own questions for use in small group discussions. When students are made aware of these different structures in expository text, their writing and comprehension improves (Raphael, Engler, & Kirschner, 1986).

In another questioning strategy that supports literacy development, Question the Author, students read narrative and informational text closely while analyzing the author's intent in the messages carried by the words. Three basic queries are initiated by asking these questions:

1. What is the author trying to say here?
2. What is the author's message?
3. What is the author talking about? (Beck, McKeown, Hamilton, & Kucan, 1997, p. 35)

By asking questions like these, the teacher can move students beyond discrete facts to larger ideas and concepts held in passages. Discussion centers around the text, rather than on memorized facts. These queries are advantageous because they prompt longer and more detailed student responses while constructing the meaning built through successive sentences, paragraphs, and chapters (Beck, McKeown, Hamilton, & Kucan, 1997). They also emphasize the voice and point of view held in any author's work, a vital skill necessary for critical analysis of information.

Discussion Strategies to Enhance Comprehension

As beads are to a necklace, so is questioning to a discussion. One of the outcomes of teaching questioning strategies is that the questions can be extended into meaningful classroom discourse. Students often have difficulty interpreting the dense informational text found in textbooks (Martin, VanCleaf, & Hodges, 1988), and discussion can help learners synthesize their prior knowledge with the new pieces of data. In this model, students construct meaning through connections to themselves, to other information sources, and to the larger world around them.

This constructivist approach values the contributions of peers in making meaning (Saunders, 1992). Effective classroom discussions place students at the center in partner and group discussions, with the teacher serving as facilitator. This is not to say that teachers allow the conversation to go in whatever direction it may. On the contrary, effective facilitation of classroom discussion demands the use of thoughtful declarative and reflective statements (Mazzoni & Gambrell, 1996) to seed the discussion and guide it when it wanders off course.

Reciprocal teaching (Palincsar & Brown, 1986) brings together questioning strategies and peer-supported learning through large and small group discussion. In reciprocal teaching, four comprehension activities—generating questions, summarizing, predicting, and clarifying—are taught within the context of a text passage. The teacher first models each of these stages, then turns the responsibility over to students. Students work in small groups of three to five members to move through the sequence (see figure 5.1). Students take turns in the role of the "teacher" or instructional leader for the small group. As students become more proficient with reciprocal teaching, they may assume a specific role, like "clarifier" or "summarizer." After completing the assigned passage, the classroom teacher once again facilitates a large group discussion of the reading, using the questions generated by the small groups. Reciprocal teaching has advantages over traditional direct explanation because it fosters procedures fluent readers use (Hermann, 1998) and allows students to capitalize on the contributions of peers to enhance their own understanding.

Effective classroom discussion is dependent on the teacher to create opportunities for content conversations to occur, as in providing reciprocal teaching events. However, some students, particularly English language learners, have difficulty with inserting themselves into the discussion. They may fear ridicule from peers or lack the habits of mind necessary for formulating a persuasive position and then sharing it with others. These students can benefit from a method of capturing a student's opinions before the discussion begins, as in the use of a discussion web.

Figure 5.1   Reciprocal Teaching Discussion Frame

BEFORE READING
Select a teacher and a recorder for this passage. The teacher will lead this portion of the reading.

The title of this passage is: _____

Predictions for this reading: _____

DURING THE READING
Read each paragraph (individually or partnered), then ask a question about the content. Answer each question as a group.

Paragraph	Question	Answer
1		
2		
3		
4		
5		

AFTER THE READING
Discuss and write a consensus of a summary for this reading.

_____

_____

_____

Discuss any confusing words or phrases.

Confusing Word or Phrase	What We Think It Means

NEXT ROTATION
Select another member of the group for the role of teacher and recorder. Begin reading the next five paragraphs of the passage.

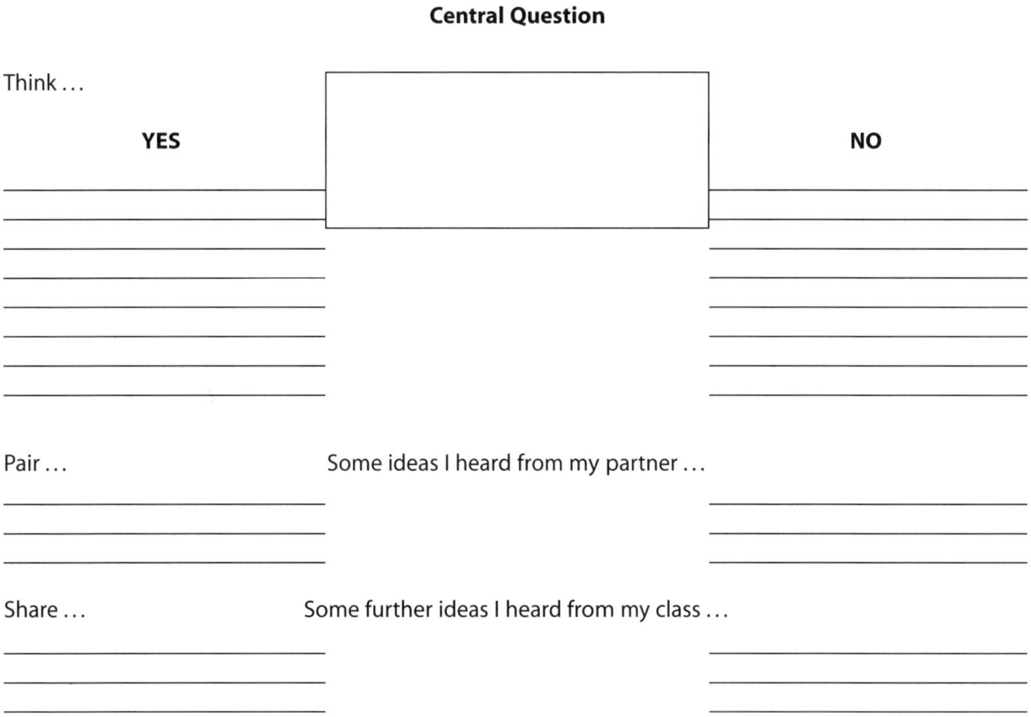

Figure 5.2   Discussion Web

Central Question

Think . . .

YES   NO

Pair . . .   Some ideas I heard from my partner . . .

Share . . .   Some further ideas I heard from my class . . .

A discussion web (Alvermann, 1991) is a graphic organizer for supporting the development and refinement of a student's opinion about a topic. It combines an organizational chart with a Think-Pair-Share (Slavin, 1989) cooperative learning process (Mazzoni & Gambrell, 1996). The teacher first presents an intriguing question to the students (one that does not have a simple yes/no answer). A worksheet for capturing ideas is distributed to each learner (see figure 5.2). Students first formulate an individual response, then pair with another classmate to begin a discussion on the focus question. Finally, the teacher invites a large group discussion of the question and records class responses on a similarly formatted chart.

In Ms. Ali's ninth grade social studies class, students used discussion webs to support their conversation about regulation of the U.S.-Mexico border. In this community, the nearby border is a source of much heated conversation, and many students have family members living on both sides. The teacher had been reading aloud the book *The Circuit* by Francisco Jimenez (1996), which tells the story of a young boy and his family surviving as migrant farm workers in central California. She first posed the question, "Should the U.S. government make it more difficult for people to enter the United States?" then had students write their impressions supporting both sides of the debate. After composing their own thoughts, students were paired to begin a discussion. In addition to sharing their own opinions, they recorded new responses forwarded by their peer. After a few minutes of paired discussion, Ms. Ali invited a class discussion of the question. She recorded their thoughts on chart paper, while students noted further salient remarks. Ms. Ali later referenced the class discussion web during their study of the history of immigration policy in the United States, noting the various arguments forwarded to support or defeat immigration legislation. She later remarked that the use of discussion webs was beneficial because it required students to note opinions that dissented from their own, and provided a structure for English language learners to support their conversations.

Textbook Feature Knowledge

In primary grades, students are exposed to a rich level of narrative text. Teachers plan instructional opportunities to discuss story frames, identify the beginning, middle, and end, and analyze characters. Students are frequently asked to retell the story in an effort to clarify understanding and gauge comprehension. However, their experiences with informational text are often limited. As noted earlier, entry into the intermediate grades marks a major shift in the type of text that is used. The importance of narrative text is increasingly balanced with the need to teach content knowledge through informational (expository) text. Yet many students have never received explicit instruction in how to access these textbooks. As with narrative, they require a deliberate and thoughtful effort to acquaint them with the strategies needed to fully extract the information lying in the pages of the textbook.

The genre of informational text differs significantly from narrative text. In addition to the dimensions discussed above, a major point of variance is the nonlinear nature of expository text (Alexander & Jetton, 2000). Unlike stories, which possess a clear time order, science and mathematics textbooks rarely possess a chronological order. Instead, they are usually constructed in a conceptual order. Readers unfamiliar with this difference in genre will approach a textbook like a story and miss the important concepts and major ideas being advanced. Indeed, it has been demonstrated that instruction in the differences in genres leads to improved student learning (Goldman & Rakestraw, 2000).

The structure of the language of the text also poses a problem for less fluent readers. Readers often expect that the first sentence of each paragraph will be the main idea (Baumann, 1986), but this is not always the case in textbooks. Depending on the nature of the author's writing style, a particular textbook may demand specific instruction on identifying the main idea. Informational text also relies more heavily on "pointer words"—the transition words that emphasize key points in the text. Examples of pointer words and phrases include *first, finally, however, in summary,* and *in other words* (Goldman & Rakestraw, 2000). These signaling devices do not contribute to the content itself, but rather are meant to direct the reader's attention to the important concepts. Instructional time devoted to identifying and interpreting pointer words and phrases can increase a reader's ability to comprehend the text, because it provides a language structure for ordering the information. An ironic note is that many so-called "remedial" textbooks eliminate these pointer words in a misguided effort to shorten sentences to reach a reduced readability quotient for struggling learners (Ciborowski, 1992).

Text features are another distinction in informational text. Narrative works rarely contain headings and subheadings, while most textbooks use these to cue readers to important topic shifts. Pictures, diagrams, and graphs are another text feature unique to expository text. While pictures are often used in stories, they only reflect the action being told by the story. In contrast, many textbooks use these items with captions to convey content. New or unfamiliar vocabulary is also introduced differently in textbooks. For instance, these words may appear in bold or italicized print, and in some textbooks a pronunciation key is also included. And of course, most textbooks feature organizational elements like a table of contents, glossary, and index. But without instruction and modeling in how to use these, many readers fail to fully comprehend.

Explicit teaching of textbook structures is warranted in all content-area classes. An excellent introduction to a new text is a book walk and scavenger hunt. A book walk is a simple lesson on the features of the textbook. Students are introduced to the major organizational features like the table of contents and index. The teacher orients the class to the structure of the textbook and interesting pictures and diagrams. After conducting a similar book walk, Ms. Chu, a fifth grade science teacher, held a textbook scavenger hunt (see figure 5.3). Students were paired, and Ms. Chu used the opportunity to observe students to determine their problem solving skills when using informational text. She said the event was such a success that she plans on using a similar activity to search for resources on the Internet.

Read Alouds

In many schools read alouds are done each day, in all content areas, at all grade levels. While this can initially prove to be a stretch for some content teachers, they quickly warm to the idea when they learn of the benefits to learners. Of particular importance is the positive effect read alouds have on attitudes and motivation toward reading (Worthy & Hoffman, 1999), and especially toward reading nonfiction (Dreher, 1998–1999). It has been shown to be effective in foreign language instruction (Richardson, 1997–1998), social studies (Irvin, Lunstrum, Lynch-Brown, & Shepard, 1995), and mathematics (Richardson, 1997). Read alouds also support language acquisition for English language learners (Amer, 1997) because it provides fluent language role models.

One of the first myths in need of squelching is the mistaken notion that read alouds can only involve narrative text (Vacca, Vacca, Prosenjak, & Burkey, 1996). While fiction and poetry can be effective additions to a content-area class, they should only be used when there is an instructional rationale for using them. Mrs. Aguilar, an eighth grade social studies teacher, reads aloud the chapter book *Number the Stars* (Lowry, 1989), a moving story of a young Danish girl whose family helps Jews escape Nazi Germany in 1943. "I find that the students relate more closely to the story of Anne Marie [the protagonist] because she's their age. Our study of World War II seems more relevant to them because they've heard the fear in Anne Marie's story." Other teachers use magazine articles, textbook passages, and newspaper clippings related to their content areas. Mr. Armstead, a

Figure 5.3   Scavenger Hunt

SCIENCE TEXTBOOK TREASURE HUNT

Group members: _____

Title of textbook: _____

ORGANIZATION
What textbook feature tells the reader the titles and pages of the chapters? _____

_____

This textbook has _____ chapters.

The glossary gives word definitions, and is on pages _____ to _____ .

The _____ is in the back of the book and tells the reader on what page a word can be found.

TEXT FEATURES
Turn to Chapter 2. What is the title? _____

List the first three headings (they are in bold capital letters).

_____   _____   _____

List the sixth, seventh, and eighth subheadings (they are in bold lowercase letters).

_____   _____   _____

How many photographs are in this chapter? _____

How many charts and graphs? _____   How many drawings? _____

Make a prediction about what you expect to learn in this chapter. _____

_____

_____

SCAVENGER HUNT: ON WHAT PAGE WOULD YOU FIND . . .

Information about satellites   _____

A photograph of a boa constrictor   _____

A diagram of the food chain   _____

A description of the Challenger accident _____

A question about tectonic plates   _____

WHO WANTS TO BE A SCIENCE MILLIONAIRE?
Use your textbook to find the answers to these questions:

The name of the green substance found in plant leaves _____

The pronunciation for the word "Sputnik" _____

The year of the San Francisco earthquake _____

The names of five simple machines

_____

_____

_____

_____

_____

TRICKS OF THE TRADE
This textbook uses words and phrases to tell you when something important is coming. Some examples are first, second, third, last, finally, in summary, in other words, and for example. Turn to any chapter that interests you, and find five of these "signal words" that tell a reader to pay attention. Write the page number, too.

Chapter title: _____

Signal Word   Page Number

_____   _____

_____   _____

_____   _____

_____   _____

_____   _____

TOO COOL FOR SCHOOL
Here are two things we found in this textbook that look pretty cool:

_____

_____

WHEN YOU'RE FINISHED
Bring this to Ms. Chu and collect your treasure!

sixth grade math teacher, used daily newspaper stories of the 2000 election vote recounts in Florida to bring the topic of statistics to life. "It just seemed like a great opportunity to show my students the importance of accurate data collection. Every day, the story continued to unfold, and I was able to create some terrific connections with the study of probability. Because the kids asked for it, we even measured the likelihood of arriving at the same figure twice when we counted and then recounted the seeds in hundreds of seed packets."

Although the possibilities in incorporating read alouds are vast, here are a few tips when using read alouds in content area classes.

1. Read alouds do not need to be long to be effective. A short, powerful passage has far more impact than a long, dull reading. Plan on about five minutes a day, and increase gradually as your students' stamina for listening improves.
2. Practice your read aloud in advance. Remember that the goal is to provide a fluent language model. That requires a bit of rehearsal so that you can bring the proper expression and inflection to the text. Think of it as a bit of a performance—you wouldn't go on stage without practicing, would you?
3. Choose readings that are meaningful to you and are connected with the course content. Comprehension increases when connections are made, so don't assume that your students understand the relevance of your selection. Be explicit about how you see the information from the selected reading fits into your course of study.
4. Determine in advance where you're going to stop. Look for the natural breaks in a piece. Selected passages can either be read in a single reading or extended over a few class periods. If the reading will continue on another day, stop at a point where you can elicit predictions about what is yet to come.

The use of read alouds in content-area classes models the importance of reading in all aspects of learning. In addition, it delivers information in a format that is accessible to all learners, because it circumvents the variable of a student's independent reading level. Finally, it allows content-area teachers to connect their discipline to the world around them, thereby demonstrating to students the relevance of their study.

Vocabulary Development

By some estimates, students acquire 3,000 new words per year (Bryant, Ugel, Hamff, & Thompson, 1999). Nagy and Anderson (1984) estimated that students are exposed to 88,500 words during their school career, far too many to teach through direct instruction. And, as many teachers can attest, a student's limited vocabulary is a major barrier to his or her comprehension of concepts and content. Students with impoverished vocabulary struggle with reading material, are limited in participating in oral language activities, and produce less sophisticated writing. These aspects of learning are keystones in any content-area class, thus infusing vocabulary and word study into lessons supports acquisition of content. However, logic dictates that the sheer volume makes the teaching of words in isolation impractical. Instead, vocabulary instruction needs to occur within context, and with a goal of helping students form their own connections, or schema, to develop a deeper understanding of the meanings conveyed by a word. Vocabulary development within the context of responsive curriculum includes word sorts, semantic feature analysis, and technical vocabulary building.

The use of word sorts often begins in primary classrooms as a way of supporting an emergent reader's word acquisition. Bear, Templeton, Invernizzi, and Johnson (1996) define word sorts as "an active process in which students categorize words" (p. 66). Students are provided with a series of pictures or words written on index cards, slips of paper, or Post-it notes. In a *closed sort*, the teacher provides a list of categories and instructs students to place words in the correct category. Ms. Eagan used the following closed word sort during her ninth grade geography class's study of Asia:

JAPAN	CHINA	VIETNAM	PHILIPPINES
yen	Changjiang	Khmer	peso
Tokyo	Beijing	Tran Du Luong	Manila
Peace Memorial	Great Wall	Mekong	Tagolog
Akihito	Forbidden City	Ho Chi Minh City	Joseph Estrada

She then has the students resort the words using new categories:

LEADERS	RIVERS	CURRENCY	CITIES	FAMOUS SITES	LANGUAGE
Tran Du Long	Changjiang	yen	Tokyo	Great Wall	Tagolog
Akihito	Mekong	peso	Beijing	Peace Memorial	
Joseph Estrada			Manila	Forbidden City	
			Ho Chi Minh City		

Ms. Eagan finds that when students have opportunities to reconceptualize characteristics of vocabulary words, they develop a deeper understanding of the words, as evidenced by their written and class discussion work.

Mr. Loaiza, the sixth grade math teacher, used an *open sort* during the first week of math in order to assess his students' understanding of mathematical concepts. An open sort differs from a closed sort in that no categories are furnished to the student; instead, each student constructs categories based on their understanding of the words. He presented students with the following mathematical terms, listed on small slips of paper and placed in an envelope:

Add	Subtract	Multiply	Divide
Product	Factor	Sum	Difference
Algebra	Arithmetic	Geometry	Negative
Angle	Circle	Acute	Prime
Zero	Perimeter	Triangle	Fraction

Mr. Loaiza circulated among the students as they worked, pausing to chat with them about their reasons for categorizing terms as they did. He made notes of each student's insights into their mathematical knowledge, and also collected each student's sorting work and their rationale for choosing their sorts. The teacher does this at the beginning of each year because he finds that his students are more relaxed about explaining their thinking than during a traditional test. "Lots of kids freeze up when the teacher says, 'OK, everyone clear off your desks and take out a pencil.' But when I have them do activities like word sorts and then talk with them about their reasoning, I get more feedback. It's like I can see their wheels turning. You can't get that from a multiple choice quiz."

Like word sorts, semantic feature analysis helps students categorize the characteristics of words in relation to one another (Anders & Bos, 1986). Students work from a grid of vocabulary words and features. Intersecting squares that represent a true statement are filled in with a "+," while those that do not possess that feature are given a "–." Semantic feature analysis grids can be further expanded to include other categories as well. Sixth grade teacher Mrs. Pham used this semantic feature analysis during her social studies unit on the History of Peace:

WORD	CONTRIBUTES TO PEACE	THREATENS PEACE	HISTORICAL EXAMPLE	CURRENT EXAMPLE
Tolerance	+	–		
Respect	+	–	Ghandi	
Prejudice	–	+		Milosevic
Bigotry	–	+	Hitler	
Patience	+	–		
Scorn	–	+		
Rapport	+	–	Eleanor Roosevelt	
Conflict	– or +	– or +		

Students used this grid throughout the unit, adding historical and modern examples as they discovered them in their course of study. Ms. Pham said the purpose of this semantic feature analysis was not to ensure that students generated a single "right" answer, but rather that they constructed and defined their own meaning. When they neared the end of the unit, she invited them to discuss their selections in groups of five. "That was a real lesson in peace for all of them! They had to listen to other people's ideas, even if they didn't agree with them. They got a firsthand experience at 'patience' and 'tolerance'!"

As Mrs. Pham noted, the true power of word sorts and semantic feature analysis is the personal investment students make in defining words (Ruddell, 1996). By revisiting their work at sorts and semantic feature analyses, they deepen their understanding of the word and its use.

The technical meanings of some vocabulary words can be a bewildering maze for some learners, and especially for those who are acquiring English as a second or third language. How can "ruler" mean one thing in history and another in math (West, 1978)? As students enter the intermediate grades, the demands for the use and understanding of technical terms increases. In mathematics, students encounter words like *prime*, *product*, and *operation*, and all require a very specific usage. Science carries an even more technical vocabulary. Words in a seventh grade science chapter about the human body included words like *tissue*, *organ*, and *vessel*. These words, and many others, carry both a common and a technical meaning. But how can we help create these connections?

A simple system used in content-area classrooms is the vocabulary notebook. In each class, students devote a section of their notebook to a vocabulary table. Through the semester, vocabulary words are recorded, along with both their common and technical definitions. A source notation is also included so that the student can refer back to an example of the word in their readings.

While Mr. Armstead, the sixth grade math teacher, used the 2000 presidential election as a way to connect students to statistical concepts, his teaching partner, Ms. Anaya, used the vocabulary notebook in her social studies class. "Mr. Armstead was doing lots of read alouds from the newspaper on the unfolding developments in Florida, but they contained lots of legal vocabulary that was new to my students. So we began collecting the common and technical definitions of the words in our notebooks. Pretty soon we had a great chart of new words." Here is a student sample.

VOCABULARY WORD	COMMON DEFINITION	TECHNICAL DEFINITION	SOURCE
party	A celebration	A political organization (Democratic, Republican, Green)	Pg. 38, social studies book
motion	To move	To ask for something in court	Article on Florida courts
hearing	To detect a sound	A court procedure to listen to both sides of an argument	ditto
landmark	A famous place	A court case that decides something new	newspaper article from 11/19/00
right	A direction or side	In politics, a person with conservative beliefs	Ms. Anaya
left	The other direction	In politics, a person with liberal beliefs	Ms. Anaya
moderate	Not too much and not too little—just right	In politics, someone who's in the middle	Ms. Anaya
chad	A boy's name	The little paper square that you poke out on a ballot	Magazine article from 11/23/00

The notebooks were helpful in Mr. Armstead's class, because he could refer students back to their notes when a newly acquired word was used in his read alouds. When an unknown word was used, students entered it into their vocabulary notebooks for later discussion with the social studies teacher. "It was really interdisciplinary in the best sense of the word," reflected Mr. Armstead.

Writing to Learn

The writing to learn strategy can be utilized across academic content areas (e.g., Andrews, 1997; Prain & Hand, 1996). This brief strategy (ten minutes or so) is introduced as a prompt, phrased as a question or sentence starter. The student spends a few minutes formulating a response, then writes for five or so minutes. Writing to learn should not be used as a summary of facts and sequences, but rather as a way to engage the learner in reflection as they make meaning of new material. The goals of writing to learn are contingent on where they are introduced during instruction. As a prereading activity, it serves to activate prior knowledge. Writing to learn during reading may be used to engage the learner in making predictions. Post-reading activities are used to extend the learner's understanding of the material by having them apply what they have learned to a new situation.

Mr. Simon uses writing to learn in his science class to provide students an opportunity to focus on the lesson for the day and to transition from their hectic passing periods between classes. While studying the respiratory system, he invited students to write in their journals about the flow of air from outside the body, through the nose or mouth, and to the blood supply.

Another writing to learn activity is called RAFT—role, audience, format, and topic (Santa & Havens, 1995). More specifically, RAFT means the following (Santa, Havens, & Harrison, 1996, p. 175):

1. The role of the writer (Who is the writer?)
2. The audience (To whom are you writing?)
3. The format (What form will it take?)
4. The topic and strong verb (What is your topic and verb?)

In traditional writing assignments, students write for the teacher as the primary audience member. RAFT assignments allow the teacher to vary any of the four dimensions of writing, which makes the writing task far more interesting for students. For example, in the science class, students may arrive from passing period and see the following on the board:

R—the respiratory system

A—oxygen

F—love letter

T—why I need you

These same students may leave their science class and arrive in their humanities class and see the following on the board:

If your last name starts with A–M	If your last name starts with N–Z
R — American colonist	**R** — British colonist
A — King George III	**A** — George Washington
F — protest letter	**F** — protest letter
T — Set us free	**T** — You belong to us

When students are first introduced to RAFT writing, the teacher provides more specific information. Over time, students will complete their RAFT assignments independently. Teachers can use RAFT as an opening for a new unit of study or as a culminating writing assignment to assess student knowledge about the topic.

Conclusion

Ensuring that students can access the text and understand the content of class discussions is vital. Teachers who use responsive curriculum design methods also understand that they can infuse literacy instruction into their teaching. While not addressing each of these instructional strategies each time they plan a lesson, over time students do experience them all. For example, all students should hear every one of their teachers read aloud regularly. Literacy is an access skill that all students must have to successfully enter the adult world. By ensuring both content knowledge and literacy skill development, teachers ensure student success.

Chapter 6

EFFECTIVE GROUPING FOR INSTRUCTION

In the United States, grouping for instruction has been dominated by a tradition of fixed ability grouping (Dewey, 1939; Dreeben & Barr, 1988; Flood, Lapp, Flood, & Nagel, 1992; Haller, 1985; Powell & Hornsby, 1993; Slavin, 1990; Soderman, Gregory, & O'Neill, 1999). In the traditional classrooms of the past, these homogeneous grouping patterns were tied to myriad difficulties, including social, emotional, and learning problems for students (e.g., DeVries & Edwards, 1974; Haller & Davis, 1980; Hiebert, 1983; Johnson, Johnson, & Maruyama, 1983; McKerrow, 1997; Spear, 1994). In order to minimize the negative effects of static grouping practices, educators and researchers have designed flexible grouping patterns (e.g., Cunningham, Hall, & Defee, 1998; Fields & Spangler, 1995; Heuwinkel, 1996; Lapp, Flood, & Ranck-Buhr, 1997). In these flexible grouping patterns, homogeneous groups are still sometimes used, but strategically, for specific instructional purposes (Indrisano & Paratore, 1991; Prawat, 1999; Swing & Peterson, 1982).

Flexible grouping practices provide a menu of patterns for teachers to implement. Whole group instruction, possibly the most prevalent configuration used in classrooms, is viewed as just one option for teaching and learning. Whole group instruction is particularly useful when introducing new material, or at the beginning of a new unit of instruction. For example, when opening a new unit on 3-D design in art, the teacher uses whole group instruction to show a collection of slides on notable collage, mixed media, and sculpture entries from the previous year's annual exhibition. But whole group instruction is limited in its effectiveness, and other configurations are necessary if the teacher is going to meet the needs of all students in today's diverse classrooms (Gamoran, 1989; Lipton & Hubble, 1997; Opitz, 1992; Slavin, 1996). The art teacher knows that other patterns are available, and uses a series of questions to make decisions about how to strategically employ both heterogeneous (mixed) and homogeneous (same) groups.

Questions to Ask When Grouping

1. What are the goals and objectives for the lesson?
    *   The goals of the lesson are the first factor is determining the best possible grouping pattern. As mentioned above, whole group instruction may work best for an introduction to a new concept or unit. However, subsequent instruction to deepen stu-

dents' understanding requires small group and partnered explorations. Thus, the goals and objectives tie the lesson plan to the grouping pattern.

2. What comprises the students' background knowledge?
   - A teacher may first select a whole group pattern in order to lead a conversation with students to determine the level of knowledge they bring to a new unit or concept. Later, homogeneous groups with student experts having in-depth topical knowledge can lead small group activities. This facilitates a shared learning experience, while promoting a student-centered classroom.

3. What is the range of student fluency in oral language?
   - Students who are acquiring English language proficiency benefit greatly from opportunities to hone their growing skills with peers. In responsive curriculum classrooms, teachers carefully place these students into small groups with a language broker who can mediate understanding within the group and provide corrective feedback.

4. What are students' interests and work habits?
   - Students possess a wide range of work habits. Some prefer working alone; others are content allowing peers to take the lead. Some students have a strong interest in the topic of study; others are only interested in completing the unit and moving on to another topic. Careful mixing of students with diverse work habits and interests creates an opportunity for modeling. These groups need careful monitoring to ensure both individual and group success.

5. Are there social concerns or needs?
   - A teacher may have a social reason for mixing a group of leaders and followers, talkers and quiet students. In such a group, each student has the chance to both receive and provide modeling for the others. These interpersonal and communication skills are reinforced through the use of group roles (recorder, spokesperson, materials manager, cheerleader) that play sometimes to a student's strengths and at other times to his or her area of need.

6. Do students have a choice?
   - At times, allowing for student choice in the selection of a partner or small group provides encouragement in accepting responsibility for their performance and work patterns. Before introducing student choice as one of the grouping configurations, create classroom community expectations that ensure that no student can be excluded or stranded without a group.

7. What are appropriate grouping formats?
   - The six common types of group configurations include: individuals, dyads or pairs, small groups of three or four students, large groups of seven to eight students, half class groups of 15 or so, and whole class grouping (Cohen, 1986, 1994; Flood et al., 1992; Reutzel, 1999; Worthy & Hoffman, 1996). These groups can be student-directed, led by the teacher, or a combination of both.

8. What materials are available?
   - The demands of a particular activity may necessitate that a particular group of students work together to access the same materials. Leveled text, in the form of books,

magazine articles, and other sources, ensures participation by all the group's members. When reading for information gathering, it is vital that students have access to text that is at their independent reading level. Text can be easily leveled by the teacher using the Fry Readability Scale (Fry, 1969). However, it is not necessary (or advisable) to place students in groups solely according their reading levels. By creating activities and providing a wide range of leveled text, each member of the group can seek source material written at his or her independent reading level, then returning to the group with the information acquired. Thus, the emphasis shifts from reading *as* a purpose to reading *for* a purpose.

- The amount of materials available can also dictate a grouping pattern. Most classrooms and school libraries possess a limited number of books on a particular topic. This can be circumvented by creating small "expert groups" to research a single aspect of a broader topic, as was done in one ninth grade science class studying the Amazon rainforest. Each group studied one issue affecting the rainforest, including deforestation, the rights of indigenous people, natural resources, current political tensions, and the biodiversity of the region. The groups then reconstituted as heterogeneous knowledge groups, with each member teaching the others about his or her topic. The use of this "jigsaw" method (Aronson, 2000) maximized finite resource materials while creating a common knowledge base on a complex topic.

Answers to these and similar questions help to provide a basis for the grouping configurations that best support instruction designed to meet students' needs. Let's take a look inside three classrooms as these various grouping configurations are implemented (e.g., Lapp, Fisher, Flood, Geiss, & Flood, 1999).

Classroom Organization of Flexible Grouping Patterns

Welcome to Kumeyaay Middle School. Students at Kumeyaay are organized into academic families of four content teachers—English, social studies, science, and math. A total of 125 students stay with their four "family" teachers throughout their middle school experience. In addition to classes taught by these four teachers, students attend a number of visual and performing arts classes over their three years in middle school. These discovery classes are sequenced according to the curriculum in sixth, seventh, and eighth grade.

We join the students of House C as they study natural disasters. Each of the teachers in House C is using the theme of natural disasters to organize the curriculum. The students have been told that they are in the middle of an emergency. They know that a major tropical depression has formed off the coast of West Africa. Will the storm intensify into a hurricane? Will it threaten valuable shipping lanes and the vulnerable southeast coastline of the United States? Should an evacuation notice be issued? Let's look inside these classrooms as the House C teachers use various grouping patterns to provide instruction.

Whole Class Instruction

Mr. Ruiz is using a variety of grouping methods to teach this interdisciplinary unit on hurricanes with his teaching partners. He begins the unit on natural disasters with a whole class discussion on storms. Mr. Ruiz uses the KWL strategy and begins class with the question "What do you think you know about storms?" The students in House C contribute various ideas including: they wreck houses, you can't sail during a storm, there are warnings for storms coming, and there are lots of kinds of storms. Mr. Ruiz then asks his students, "What do you want to know about storms?" This questions causes a flurry of conversation. The students in House C want to know about the causes of storms, how to detect their arrival, how to prevent them, and what to do during an emergency. Mr. Ruiz then provides the whole class with a journal prompt, providing students with new journals to use for the storm unit and inviting them to make the first entry. "Thinking About Storms" is the title of the first journal entry. Mr. Ruiz ends this whole class session with a read aloud of *Eye of the Storm: Chasing Storms with Warren Faidley* (Kramer, 1997).

Learning Stations and Centers

Later during the week, Mr. Ruiz provides his science class with content information about storms using the Center Activity Rotation System (CARS) (Lapp, Flood, & Goss, 2000). Within this rotation system, students are divided into heterogeneous, cooperative groups. Each of the groups works at one of four learning stations designed to build background knowledge, using a four-day rotation. Mr. Ruiz has designed one station to focus on the deadliest hurricane in United States history, the Galveston storm of 1906. At this station, he has provided various print and non-print materials and a list of questions about the Galveston storm. At a second station, Mr. Ruiz bookmarked an interactive site sponsored by the Discovery Channel on a classroom computer so that students could create their own hurricane by manipulating variables like humidity, water temperature, and wind shear (http://www.discovery.com/stories/science/hurricanes/create.html), and then compare the hurricane they created with other real hurricanes. A third station includes tracking maps displaying the paths of major storms over the last century. The fourth station features information about evacuation timetables in the coastal areas of the Southeast. Additionally, Mr. Ruiz daily works at a teacher center with a small, homogeneous group on reading and discussing leveled text passages on hurricanes to provide information through direct, explicit teaching. Mr. Ruiz also meets with individual students as needed. On the fifth day students work at the center that they missed while they were at the teacher center, and Mr. Ruiz circulates through the groups to gather informal assessment information. Students at each of the learning stations use their journals to record information about the lesson and respond to questions that are raised by the teacher and their peers.

Cooperative Grouping

In Ms. Weiss's social studies class, students in House C work in small cooperative, heterogeneous groups (Antil, Jenkins, Wayne, & Vadasy, 1998; Flood, Lapp, & Wood, 1998; Johnson & Johnson, 1994) to study charts, maps, and graphs for information about four major twentieth-century hurricanes. Many of the students are English language learners, so oral fluency is always a consideration when designing groups. One of her goals is to have students interact with one another and share information because she believes this supports the development of language fluency. She has found that the use of language brokers during cooperative groups adds a level of support. Each of the students in the cooperative group has an assignment, such as recorder, timekeeper, and facilitator, to complete the day's task of researching hurricanes through history, including Donna, 1960; Camille, 1969; Hugo, 1989; and Andrew, 1992. These heterogeneous groups will later report on their storm to the class. Ms. Weiss likes the cooperative groups to share what they have learned as a whole class because it provides an accountability piece for each group and contributes to the overall knowledge base. As the small groups work, Ms. Weiss walks around the room, listens in on each group, provides direct instruction, and answers questions in order to ensure that all students receive individualized instruction.

Individuals and Partners

In Mr. Jimenez's English class, students are reading the novel *The Silent Storm* (Garland, 1995). Mr. Jimenez often reads a chapter aloud and then invites students to read the next chapter with a partner. He believes that these partner reading experiences encourage conversations between students and deepens their understanding of the character, plot, and story. He also knows that these partner conversations allow students to "move into the novel" and result in much richer responses to literature.

In addition to the time spent reading, Mr. Jimenez uses partner activities in reviewing the language used in the book. Student teams are assigned an area of expertise and listen as their teacher reads. Some partners listen for unique vocabulary words, while others listen for "golden phrases," clues about the characters, setting descriptions, or historical connections. At the end of the read aloud or partner reading, each team shares with the whole class the information they gathered. All students keep running logs on each of these categories in their journals.

Small Groups

Our next stop is with Mrs. Chang, a sixth grade math teacher. Here we see students working on their culminating project, studying a developing storm created by Mr. Ruiz, and utilizing changing charts and graphs of the storm, provided by Ms. Weiss. Each group must issue media releases for the public regarding warnings, evacuation notices, and news stories. Small hetergeneous groups of four craft their responses based on the data. While they are doing so, Mrs. Chang meets with individuals to discuss their work. She uses student-teacher conferences to offer small group instruction to her students. She believes that this individualized attention has resulted in significant gains in student achievement and motivation.

Summary

Although permanent ability groups may have been the preferred instructional format for teaching in the past, growing evidence and current practices have demonstrated that student needs can be met through flexible grouping structures. Every instructional episode must be carefully considered so that grouping can be planned effectively. We must be careful to match student needs with the most appropriate group experience. The teachers at Kumeyaay Middle School have demonstrated a variety of ways that students can be effectively grouped for instruction.

Chapter 7

USING TECHNOLOGY AS A LEARNING TOOL

The use of instructional technology has become an expected skill for high school graduates (see figure 7.1 for the National Educational Technology Standards). The workplace today requires that employees be familiar with a variety of types of technology. Teachers must understand how to meaningfully use technology as an instructional tool. This chapter highlights the technology-related activities and assignments that can be used to support students. In addition, the chapter provides information regarding the ways in which teachers are addressing the technology standards.

During the past decade, the number of computers used in classrooms has significantly increased. In 1997, schools averaged one computer for every six students nationwide (*Education Week*, 1998); ten years ago there was approximately one computer for 30 students. The annual budget for school computers topped $5 billion last year (*Education Week*, 1998). Healy (1998) maintains a need to assess the impact of computers and technology on student literacy as schools attempt to expand the numbers of computers per classroom. We must determine if, in fact, computers improve literacy. Healy (1999) also explains that we need to understand a complex set of issues, including when computers should be introduced into our classrooms and what computer activities are most beneficial for students. It may very well be, as Reinking (1998) noted, that "questions about whether students using word processing write as well or better than those using conventional materials have given way to questions about how students might adapt to and employ effectively electronic forms of reading and writing" (p. xxiv).

We now turn to a discussion of three potential uses of technology in the classroom: writing instruction, electronic literacy environments, and electronic portfolios.

Writing Instruction

Dahl and Farnan (1998) point out in their book *Children's Writing*, that computers and technology have significantly altered the ways in which people experience the world. Researchers have attempted to document positive outcomes when students use computers as part of their writing process program. As Dahl and Farnan note, the research results are complex. For example, Russell (1991), in her meta-analysis, found that the relationship between technology and writing was significantly influenced by the social interactions that students had in the computer lab, although the writing was higher quality when students used word processing software and computers.

Figure 7.1   National Educational Technology Standards

1. Basic operations and concepts
   - Students demonstrate a sound understanding of the nature and operation of technology systems.
   - Students are proficient in the use of technology.

2. Social, ethical, and human issues
   - Students understand the ethical, cultural, and societal issues related to technology.
   - Students practice responsible use of technology systems, information, and software.
   - Students develop positive attitudes toward technology uses that support lifelong learning, collaboration, personal pursuits, and productivity.

3. Technology productivity tools
   - Students use technology tools to enhance learning, increase productivity, and promote creativity.
   - Students use productivity tools to collaborate in constructing technology-enhanced models, prepare publications, and produce other creative works.

4. Technology communications tools
   - Students use telecommunications to collaborate, publish, and interact with peers, experts, and other audiences.
   - Students use a variety of media and formats to communicate information and ideas effectively to multiple audiences.

5. Technology research tools
   - Students use technology to locate, evaluate, and collect information from a variety of sources.
   - Students use technology tools to process data and report results.
   - Students evaluate and select new information resources and technological innovations based on the appropriateness for specific tasks.

6. Technology problem-solving and decision-making tools
   - Students use technology resources for solving problems and making informed decisions.
   - Students employ technology in the development of strategies for solving problems in the real world.

Source: National Educational Technology Standards. Available at: http://cnets.iste.org/index.html.

In a study of first graders' use of word processing software, Jones and Pellegrini (1996) found that the technology facilitated the students' writing of narratives. These researchers hypothesized that the use of the computer shifted the focus away from the mechanical aspects of writing and toward words and ideas. More specifically, computers allow students to focus more directly on words and ideas than on handwriting, letter formation, and alignment of words.

Similar results have been documented for older students as well. In their study of middle school students, Owston, Murphy, and Wideman (1992) found that students wrote higher quality essays using word processing software than when they wrote their essays in cursive. All the students in their study were experienced computer users. The researchers hypothesized that the reason for the high quality was related to the number of times students revised their work on the computer. Odenthal (1992) found similar results among second language learners. Haas (1989) documented similar results; she found that easy-to-use software programs facilitated the revision process. The results of these studies indicate that technology:

1. helps children to focus on content rather than mechanics,
2. encourages the production of more and better developed essays, and
3. reduces the drudgery of editing.

Electronic Literacy Environments

Research indicates a positive relationship between electronic environments and literacy (Baines, 1998; Beach & Lundell, 1998; Kieffer, Hale, & Templeton, 1998). Reading and writing in an electronic literacy environment differs from traditional classroom activities. Typically, when students are asked to write papers, they know their audience and the expectations of the teacher. However, in writing something for the web that anyone can read, students "place a premium on the paper's accuracy, use of technical and specialized vocabulary, and degree of coherence" (Alvarez, 1998, p. 45).

In addition to publishing on the World Wide Web, a number of electronic conversations can be facilitated. Students can establish two kinds of conversations: asynchronous, such as email, or synchronous, such as chat rooms. Participants in these conversations are required to access prior knowledge, read strings of messages, provide written responses, and master the technology. All of these are useful skills and relate to overall literacy development. Interestingly, most students report enjoying the experience because, unlike face-to-face conversations, they are not interrupted when constructing their responses (Beach & Lundell, 1998).

For example, Garner and Gillingham (1998) describe a series of Internet interactions among students. In a year-long partnership, students in two classrooms are introduced, thus providing an opportunity for Yup'ik Eskimo children and adolescents to practice speaking, reading, and writing their second language, English. The authors note that bilingualism was important to this village, located 300 miles from the nearest road. The Internet was one of the few places that English could be practiced authentically and comfortably. The teachers observed significant progress for both groups of students, noting "unity of expression, increased grammatical competence, and improvement in the mechanics of spelling, capitalization, and punctuation" (p. 223). These studies demonstrate that accessing electronic literacy environments produces:

1. increased specialized vocabulary and coherence,
2. wide ranging possibilities for communication and expression, and
3. improved mechanics of writing.

Electronic Portfolios

Authentic assessments, such as portfolios, have been a significant focus for assessment professionals and teachers during the past decade (Flippo, 1997; Valencia, Hiebert, & Afflerbach, 1994). The need to document learning and progress beyond standardized tests and the desire to showcase exemplary pieces of student work has provided the impetus for new types of portfolios (Kieffer & Morrison, 1994). Portfolios can look like scrapbooks, folders, photo albums, or file cabinets.

As a result, a number of electronic versions of portfolios have been developed. Some of them are preprogrammed, such as the Grady Profile (Grady, 1991). Others are developed by professional organizations or teachers. For example, the Annenberg Institute for School Reform and the Coalition of Essential Schools have been investigating digital portfolios and software programs that create a multimedia collection of student work (Niguidula, 1995). Still others require that students create their own versions by using word processing and multimedia software (Kieffer, Hale, & Templeton, 1998).

Electronic portfolios require that students access technology while demonstrating their personal growth. Students can collect artifacts for their portfolios and align them with the performance standards of the school (Fisher, Sax, & Jorgensen, 1998). For example, students may be expected to demonstrate their ability to read, write, speak, and listen for a variety of purposes and audiences. Their portfolios should contain evidence, across grade levels, that they accomplished this standard. Some students will choose to store electronic versions of text in their portfolios. Others will scan photos, sound clips, or video clips into a software program for later use. Still others will use multimedia authoring software and CD-ROMs to increase the interactivity the reviewer has with the contents.

In a recent study of the outcomes of electronic portfolios, Hedberg (1998) studied 60 high school students. He documented increased knowledge of technology, increased literacy skills, and increased interest in science when his students were required to maintain and submit electronic portfolios of their work. He hypothesizes that the effect of electronic portfolios is due in large part to the increase in ownership and pride by students. He notes that students in his classes had basic computer skills and most could type. Again, the implications for teachers are clear—students need access to computers, word processing software, and keyboarding if they are to participate in many of these electronic literacy events. These studies demonstrate that the use of electronic portfolios:

1. encourage students to align their school work with performance standards,
2. provide an opportunity for students to share their literacy development with others,
3. increase knowledge of technology, and
4. improve literacy overall.

Classroom Uses of Technology

Integrating technology into classroom activities often provides additional motivation for students. Technology also offers a wider range of instructional approaches that meet the diverse learning needs of students. In addition to the three ideas just presented, many of the following activities offer initial steps toward expanding the use of technology as a learning tool.

Book Club Discussions

Book clubs offer a wealth of opportunities for students to read, write, interpret, react, predict, and share ideas with their peers about literature (Flood, Lapp, & Fisher, 1999). Book Club activities can be enhanced by including an online discussion that enables students to post late-breaking thoughts, new insights, or ideas that they felt awkward presenting in

Figure 7.2   Glossary of Technology Terms

Chat room A web place that allows for synchronous discussions. People all log on at the same time and engage in a conversation—although in written form.

Cookies An electronic "packet" of information that is collected when subscribing on a website; typically includes a person's name, address, email, and other identifying information.

Discussion board A web place that allows for discussions that are saved electronically. The discussion does not have to be synchronous (occurring at the same time). People can log onto the discussion board at any time and contribute to the conversation.

Email Electronic mail, a way to send a message to somebody else on the Internet (used as both a noun and a verb).

Emoticon Using a combination of symbols available on a keyboard to express an emotion, e.g., =) for happy, =(for sad, =0 for surprise (turn the page sideways to see the face).

Listserv A brand-name software often used generically to describe a tool for distributing messages to a list of subscribers who have a shared interest in a topic, who are in a class together, or for some other purpose. A message sent to the listserv is received by everyone who is subscribed via specific commands written to a list manager.

Search engine A tool used to look for a topic or specific website by typing in keywords. Search engines typically go through about 5% of the Internet and then list all matching websites. Search engines include Yahoo!, AltaVista, Lycos, Google, and Excite, to name a few.

Spam Junk mail on the Internet; can include unsolicited advertising, chain letters, and viruses (which can cause problems with the function of the computer).

Surfing (as in "surfing the web") Refers to spending time looking at websites, typically includes going from one to another, checking out new sites by clicking on links (other addresses) listed on another website, or going to new sites via search engines

Website A page of information on the Internet that can be found by typing in the URL (universal resource locator, i.e., address) or by using a search engine to type in keywords. For example, most commercial and nonprofit companies all have their own websites to advertise or describe their mission, services, products and so forth.

person. A simple discussion board format can be created on a class website for students to access on an individual basis (see figure 7.2 for a discussion of common technology terms). All discussions are asynchronous, that is, posted at any time (versus setting up a specific time to participate in a "real time" chat). The responses remain on the board, so that anyone logging on to post a message can read the previous messages. This is particularly beneficial for students who may need more time to compose their ideas before sharing with their classmates. If necessary, students have the opportunity to write their responses in a word processing program and edit their writing before copying and pasting it into the discussion board.

In a ninth grade English class, Mr. DeVon wanted his students to consider unrequited love and classist beliefs while they read Romeo and Juliet. He arranged for in-class discussions of the play as well as interactive journals in which he and his individual students could discuss the themes. Mr. DeVon noticed that the addition of the web-based discussion board allowed his shyer and quieter students to participant in conversations and share their reflections on the book and the class themes. In addition, Mr. DeVon noticed that students from different class periods began discussing the play. He realized that this could never happen given the structure of the current school schedule. Finally, when Mr. De-Von analyzed the conversations on the web versus conversations in class, he understood that he was not the primary audience for the discussion board conversation, whereas he was the primary audience for the classroom discussions.

WebQuests

A WebQuest is an inquiry-oriented activity in which some or all of the information with which learners interact comes from resources on the internet, optionally supplemented with videoconferencing (Dodge, 1995). WebQuests are deliberately designed to make the best use of a learner's time. As educators, we often question the educational value of inviting students to "surf the net" without a clear task in mind. WebQuests are a structured way to facilitate learning via the World Wide Web and should contain at least the following parts (Dodge, 1997):

*   An introduction that sets the stage and provides some background information.
*   A task that is doable and interesting.
*   A set of information sources needed to complete the task. Many (though not necessarily all) of the resources are embedded in the WebQuest document itself as anchors pointing to information on the World Wide Web. Information sources might include web documents, experts available via email or real-time conferencing, searchable databases on the net, and books and other documents physically available in the learner's setting. Because pointers to resources are included, the learner is not left to wander through webspace completely adrift.
*   A description of the process the learners should go through in accomplishing the task. The process should be broken out into clearly described steps.
*   Some guidance on how to organize the information acquired. This can take the form of guiding questions or directions to complete organizational frameworks, such as timelines, concept maps, or cause-and-effect diagrams.
*   A conclusion that brings closure to the quest reminds the learners about what they've learned and perhaps encourages them to extend the experience into other domains.

A WebQuest typically is organized into several categories. These are often found on a website that the teacher has created, thus allowing links to additional resources and making them more accessible. The WebQuest model usually involves the following: introduction, task, resources, process, evaluation, and conclusion. There are a number of WebQuests already available at the website: http://edweb.sdsu.edu/webquest/webquest .html. This site encourages new submissions of WebQuests and has been growing exponentially since 1995.

Figure 7.3 provides students with a list of criteria for evaluating websites. Teachers such as Mr. Wagner have added evaluation forms such as these for both print and web-based information sources. Mr. Wagner knows that his 8th grade science students will be ex-

Figure 7.3   Evaluation of Web-based Information

EVALUATION OF WEB DOCUMENTS	HOW TO INTERPRET THE BASICS
1. Accuracy of web documents • Who wrote the page and can you contact him or her? • What is the purpose of the document and why was it produced? • Is this person qualified to write this document?	Accuracy • Make sure author provides e-mail or a contact address/phone number. • Know the distinction between author and webmaster.
2. Authority of web documents • Who published the document and is it separate from the "webmaster"? • Check the domain of the document, what institution publishes this document?	Authority • What credentials are listed for the author(s)? • Where is the document published? • Check URL domain.
3. Objectivity of web documents • What goals/objectives does this page meet? • How detailed is the information? • What opinions (if any) are expressed by the author?	Objectivity • Determine if page is a mask for advertising; if so information might be biased. • View any web page as you would an infomercial on television. Ask yourself why was this written and for whom?
4. Currency of web documents • When was it produced? • When was it updated? • How up-to-date are the links (if any)?	Currency • How many dead links are on the page? • Are the links current or updated regularly? • Is the information on the page outdated?
5. Coverage of the web documents • Are the links (if any) evaluated and do they complement the document's theme? • Is it all images or a balance of text and images? • Is the information presented cited correctly?	Coverage • If page requires special software to view the information, how much are you missing if you don't have the software? • Is it free, or is there a fee to obtain the information? • Is there an option for text only, or frames, or a suggested browser for better viewing?

Source: Jim Kapoun, reference and instruction librarian at Southwest State University, *College and Research Libraries News* (July/August, 1998): 522–523. Available at: http://servercc.oakton.edu/~wittman/find/eval.htm.

posed to pseudo-science, pop science, and authentic science information in magazines, books, and on the web. He uses these evaluation forms to ensure that his students have a way to critically analyze the information they find while researching in his class.

Debates/Opinion Polls

Many teachers use debates to help students examine their own values, attitudes, opinions, or experiences on a specific topic. A debate could be virtual and available for a week or two, giving the students the opportunity to log on with their opinions on a given controversy, such as the one in Ms. Johnson's science class, "Should the federal government continue to fund cloning?"

Posting a survey via a web form online may be a way for students to complete a paper-less opinion poll. This format introduces students to the use of web forms, which are becoming more and more common as a way to order everything from airplane reservations to groceries. Students could also share the website with others to poll a wider audience (of other classes or schools) and learn how to tally the answers with the use of appropriate software. For example, the students in Mr. Arenal's art class wanted to know more about their peers' understanding of aesthetics. They collected a number of websites that contained famous turn-of-the-century paintings. Their survey form required students to rate the painting on a number of characteristics, including how well the painting captured the viewers' interest.

Letter Writing

As students learn how to write different types of letters, they can be introduced to the use of templates on the computer. Software programs such as Microsoft Word include a variety of these, which can be found when opening a new file document. (Click on File, New, then choose from Letters & Faxes, Memos, Other Documents, and Web Pages.) Templates can also be customized to create personal letterhead, class stationery, or similar purposes. Students can access these templates and just fill in required information. Letters can then be printed and mailed by traditional "snail mail" or could be attached to an email message. Writing letters to relatives, friends, classmates, or teachers via the computer offers students a different way to communicate and also to become familiar with a variety of letter formats and their uses. Students can take advantage of spell-check and grammar-check before completing the letter.

In Mrs. Kumar's civics class, students were expected to use the word processing software to complete a number of correspondence requirements. For example, they had to attend a public meeting and produce meeting minutes and compare their minutes with those published. Her students were also asked to write letters to governmental agencies suggesting actions be taken about social justice issues they were studying (e.g., homelessness, drug abuse, HIV/AIDS education, support for public libraries, institutionalization of persons with mental retardation). Finally, Mrs. Kumar's students used their knowledge of word processing and letter writing to invite elected officials to their school for the opening of the new health center.

Email Correspondence

Comparing and contrasting the format for letters and memos with the format of the email message helps students clarify the appropriateness of each. Just as spoken language inside the classroom is different from the language that students use at lunch or in their neighborhoods, written language must also be adapted to the environment. Setting up a class listserv for students to send email messages to one another or to the whole class can be integrated as part of many curricular activities (i.e., to share predictions, reactions, or other comments on a particular lesson). It can also be used to replace the traditional "passing notes in class" communication. Students may want to build a glossary of "emoticons" and their meanings so that everyone understands this new cyber-language. For example, using a sideways smile, =), is often used to signify a joke or sarcasm, and a frown, :(, is used to express displeasure, acknowledgement of something sad, or an apology. Many abbreviations are also used in email such as IMHO (in my humble opinion), LOL (laughing out loud), and TIA (thanks in advance).

Beyond emailing their teacher, students in Ms. Greene's journalism class use email and email attachments to communicate with people who they want to interview. They also send regular PDF (portable document format) files to one another to review layout and formats. Ms. Greene has also provided each of her students with access to an E-Pal (electronic pen pal) in another country so that they can report on "first person" stories from around the world. She used the KeyPals website (http://www.keypals.com/) to locate appropriate matches for her students. Finally, Ms. Greene sends all of her reminders and homework assignments to her students via email. She finds this especially useful given their journalism schedule and the deadlines they face in producing a high quality student newspaper.

Multimedia Presentations

When doing reports or other classroom presentations, students can use software such as Powerpoint™ or Illustrator™ to represent their ideas. Easy to use, these programs can include pictures, graphs, tables, and more, and can be shown in a slide show format. Powerpoint™ offers a view of all the slides so that the sequence can be rearranged as necessary. Using this same feature, a teacher might use slides to give previews of a story as an anticipatory set, provide pieces of a story that the students could sequence correctly, or offer different endings to a story that the students would complete.

Students in Mr. Clark's world history classes use multimedia presentations to share information about World War II with their peers. Mr. Clark has students work in cooperative groups on a number of different topics. Students work in groups to search the World Wide Web, textbooks, library reference books, and films for information and pictures about their topic. Mr. Clark presents information about World War II in a chronological fashion, from the depression through reconstruction. Approximately two weeks into the unit, Mr. Clark played a recording of the bombing of Pearl Harbor. A group of students then became the instructors and shared the information that they had gathered with the whole class. This group had scanned a series of photos from the National Archives into their Powerpoint™ presentation and used actual quotes from eyewitnesses as their narration. A few days later, the class learned of the atomic bombing of Japan. The student group read aloud the book *Faithful Elephants* (Tsuchiya, 1951) and then shared photos of Peace Park in Hiroshima gathered via the Internet. They focused on the story of *Sadako* (Coerr, 1993) and shared the making of paper cranes. This group invited their peers to visit the Sadako website at www.sadako.com. As the students in Mr. Clark's class presented their research, they became experts in their assigned part of history. Throughout the unit, students would reference back to the visual information gathered within their group and make connections to other parts of their World War II study.

Figure 7.4   Sample Webliography Format

URL: _____

1. Title of website: _____

2. What's the main purpose of the site? _____

   _____

   • Is it selling something?
   • Does it describe a service?
   • Is it an educational site?

3. Who created the site? _____

   • Is there a contact name?
   • Is it a private company?
   • Is it a school?
   • Is it a government agency?

4. How current is the site? (When was it last updated?) _____
   (This should be listed at the bottom of the home page.)

5. Are links available to other sites? Do they really link? (try at least some of them) _____

   _____

   (These are often listed as: Links, Resources, Other Websites)

6. Accessibility
   • Is the site user-friendly? (easy to figure out, follow, find information)
   • Is site available in graphics and text only options? (This is helpful to know if you have students who are blind and use a screen-reading software.)

7. What did you learn from this site?

   _____

   _____

   _____

Webliography

This activity provides students with an opportunity to describe and critique the websites that they find on a specific topic. The webliography is similar to an annotated bibliography. There is some freedom in searching, similar to looking for books or magazine articles. However, the search is limited to a specific topic. The product is a list of web resources that can be shared with members of the class. Typically students report the following features: ease of navigation through the site; appropriateness to the subject area; links to related sites; and the use of graphics, pictures, sounds, or alternative formats. Figure 7.4 provides a format that students can use to collect websites for their webliography.

Mrs. Atkins invited her students to complete webliographies on famous composers for their middle school general music class. Students worked in groups to find information about composers such as Bach, Handel, Mozart, Beethoven, Chopin, Brahms, and Joplin. Mrs. Atkins posted all the webliographies on her music education website for students to access. As each group presented their webliographies, she read aloud from the book *Meet the Great Composers* (Montgomery & Hinson, 1995) and played a selection of each composer's work from the CD that accompanies the book.

Conclusions

We offer a qualified yes to the question, "Are computers a welcome addition to the classroom?" When computers and other forms of technology are used as an instructional tool by teachers who have received appropriate training and support, the money is well spent. However, the lack of appropriate staff development can result in expensive equipment sitting unused. Computers will be a part of the twenty-first century, and our students will use them for a variety of reasons including Internet access, writing, record keeping, and email. With support, teachers can add this powerful tool to the host of instructional strategies they use to engage students in meaningful instruction.

Chapter 8

FOCUS ON DIVERSE LEARNERS

The schools of the twenty-first century bustle with promise of the future, a future enriched by the diversity of today's students. An exuberant mix of cultures and languages, abilities and talents weaves a tapestry of learning in classrooms that maximize this potential. As with all great possibilities, there is the shadow of failure as well. Schools with diverse student populations, particularly many urban schools, face challenges that mirror the difficulties of the larger society—hunger, neglect, low expectations, even lower self-image, division, and marginalization. Schools have long been viewed as the emergency room of society—a place where the ills of the community are to be bandaged and treated. But triage is not teaching, and treatment is not learning.

The population of a school reflects the community, and its classrooms should as well. The diversity of a school is most often viewed through the three lenses—English language learners, students identified as gifted or talented, and students with disabilities. These students bring to the classroom their unique talents as well as their support needs. In the past, the prevailing practice was to isolate these learners into discrete groups, in a mistaken belief that a specialized system of supports could then be implemented. However, decades of research have proven that the outcomes do not match the promises. The relationship between ability grouping and pedagogy must be recognized. Nieto (1996) writes

> Students in the lowest levels, for example, are most subjected to rote memorization and worn methods, as their teachers often feel that these are the children who need, first, to master the "basics." Until the basics are learned, the thinking goes, creative methods are a frill that these students can ill afford. Poor children and those most alienated by the schools are once again the losers. The cycle of school failure is repeated: The students most in need are placed in the lowest-level classes and exposed to the drudgery of drill and repetition; school becomes more boring and senseless every day, and the students become discouraged and drop out. (p. 89)

Students identified as gifted have benefited from excellent instruction; the failed promise is in who has been excluded, and in the damage done to a school community when students are separated from their peers. In gifted education, outstanding curriculum design approaches have been developed and implemented, including differentiated instruction (Tomlinson, 1999) and multiple intelligences (Gardner, 1983). But traditional gifted education approaches have failed to overcome the underrepresentation of African-Americans (Ford, 1998; Harris & Ford, 1999; Sisk, 1994), Hispanics and Latinos (Strom, 1990), Native Americans (Romero, 1994), English language learners (Peterson & Margolin, 1997), and students with disabilities (Baum, Olenchak, & Owen, 1998; Hiatt & Covington, 1991); gender imbalance is an issue, as well (Sadker, 1999). And most educators are in agreement that these are the students most at-risk, and most in need of excellent supports. Doesn't it make sense, then, that well-designed curricular supports are made available to all students, thus circumventing this history of underrepresentation?

School communities suffer when students identified as gifted are singled out for special and often inequitable education. A powerful and destructive message is conveyed to all students when a school endorses the blatant hierarchy of competitive achievement that pits one student against another (Sapon-Shevin, 1994a). As Sapon-Shevin (1994b) notes, separate, "gifted-only" classes disrupt the sense of community on a school campus and serves as a continual reminder of individual worth.

Students with disabilities have also encountered barriers to equity and excellence. Although public schools were designed to provide free and appropriate public education for all students, students identified with disabilities have not always received the same type of education as their peers without disabilities. A continuum of placements was designed to provide a full range of services for individuals with disabilities, from the most restrictive to the least restrictive environments. At one time, a common practice dictated placing individuals with disabilities who required the most intense services in the most restrictive environment, separating them from their same-age peers (Department of Education, 1999). Educators now see that separate education often results in social exclusion in school and the community, acquisition of inappropriate behavior, and an inability to generalize knowledge to new environments (Yell, Rogers, & Rogers, 1998). Further, students without disabilities grew up without the experience of knowing peers with disabilities, leaving them ill-prepared to become friends, neighbors, employers, coworkers, parents of individuals with disabilities, or individuals with disabilities themselves (Fisher, Pumpian, & Sax, 1998). Thus, inclusive education has become part of many school reform efforts, impacting not only schools, but also the community (Kennedy & Fisher, 2001).

An inclusive education offers students with disabilities the opportunity to apply functional skills in the general education classroom while also accessing the curriculum standards alongside their peers. Inclusion is typically thought of as the placement of students with disabilities in their neighborhood schools in general education classrooms with peers their own age (NASBE, 1995). Caution must be taken to provide appropriate supports and services in these classrooms for students to be included, versus letting them be "dumped" without support. Coordinating supports and accommodations is necessary for success; indeed, we owe it to all students. The wise practices of inclusive education can serve many students in responsive curriculum classrooms.

In terms of English language learners, we know that many students who are learning English as a second language do not receive their education in a bilingual classroom or from a bilingual teacher. This may be because of the lack of available personnel, the number of students representing the specific language group, or pressures from politicians and public debate (August & Hakuta, 1998). As a result, many students who are learning English are educated in the "low" group and spend a significant amount of their instructional time with remedial work (Dugan & Desir, 1998). Fortunately, there is a great deal of information available about "sheltered" class instruction for English language learners in mainstream classes (e.g., Faltis & Wolfe, 1998; Watts-Taffe & Truscott, 2000). While not replacing the need for quality bilingual education, students who are learning English and who are enrolled in content classes require support to be in order successful.

The fields of gifted education, special education, and second language acquisition offer excellent supports for all learners, not just those identified as possessing a set of characteristics. Compacting, interest groups, and tiered assignments and tests are traditionally gifted practices; Total Physical Response and realia are most often associated with second language acquisition; and accommodations/modifications and scaffolding are usually offered to students with IEPs (Individual Educational Plan). We discuss these practices, as well as writing prompts and concept maps, in this discussion of techniques for supporting all learners in responsive curriculum classrooms. Let's take a tour of some eighth grade classrooms to see how these strategies are used to support diverse learners.

Middle School Meets the Middle Ages

The eighth grade at Chavez Middle School is waiting for a Renaissance. Not an educational one—that has been happening here for the past decade, as the school has engaged in a whole school reform effort based on equity and excellence for all its students. Block scheduling began seven years ago, gifted classes were absorbed five years back, and the last of the special education classes was closed three years ago. The school has assembled a track record of success with its innovative approach to supporting diverse learners. The entire school is untracked, meaning that students are not channeled into remedial, average, and honors classes. Instead, all classes are heterogeneously grouped, and individual supports for students identified as gifted (and for that matter, not identified) are negotiated through independent contracts. Four teachers are assigned to each "house" and 90 students attend classes together. A special educator serves as a support to this house.

The Renaissance CMS is awaiting is the one that marked an era of tremendous growth in Europe. You see, the eighth grade is in the midst of a two-week interdisciplinary look at the Middle Ages. The unit was designed two years ago through the collaborative efforts of the teachers in the Respeto house. (Respeto is the Spanish word for "respect"—each eighth grade house has adopted a name that reflects the core values of the school's mission statement.) Ms. Caufield is the science teacher, Mr. Amante teaches English, Mrs. Park is the social studies instructor, and Mr. Tabers teaches mathematics. The house also receives the support of Ms. Duong, the special education teacher. The Respeto teachers named this unit "Middle School Meets the Middle Ages" because they felt is was important for the students to experience what life was like for their peers during that time in history.

Realia

Imagine that you have never seen a castle or a knight in shining armor. How difficult would this lack of experience make your understanding of the Middle Ages? Realia provides learners with an example of the topic or word under study (Lapp, Fisher, & Flood, 1999). Realia can be authentic photos, tangible items, or replications of distinct parts of a larger item. For example, a science teacher often uses a human skeleton to discuss the human bone structure. This same science teacher may use photographs, images, or plastic models of the brain and central nervous system. Regardless, the realia provided in these lessons builds learners' confidence in their language abilities, makes language learning more relevant, contextualizes the learning, and prepares learners for post-classroom experiences.

In the study of the Middle Ages, Mr. Amante read aloud the book *Marguerite Makes a Book* (Robertson, 1999). Mr. Amante noticed that many of his students had difficulty with several of the ideas presented in this text, including illuminated manuscript, parchment, and quill. To improve their comprehension, Mr. Amante brought samples of each of these items to class for the students to see and touch. In addition, he talked with the art teacher, and together they decided that students should mix colors, make paper, and create their own illuminated manuscripts.

Total Physical Response (TPR)

Total Physical Response is a language development methodology based on the coordination of speech and action developed by James Asher (1996). TPR has been in use for nearly thirty years. While other methods have come and gone, TPR is still a valuable tool when teaching English language learners (and others for whom language is difficult, such as students with learning disabilities). Despite the wealth of materials available to us, nothing is more useful than this very direct and visual instruction.

With the TPR method, the teacher says a single action word or phrase such as "stand up" or "put the paper on the table" and then demonstrates the action. At first, students will only be able to follow the command. They may also be able to repeat the teacher's words as they copy the action. The next step is to proceed to more difficult language while still keeping the instruction direct and visual. Many teachers use simple TPR sequences in order to enlarge the students' vocabulary, teach the present continuous and past tense in context, and practice English sentence structure and word order.

When Ms. Caufield uses TPR to provide science lab instructions, she tapes her instructions with background music. This gives her the opportunity to repeat the command, demonstrate the action, and not worry about what command to do next. She can be sure that she has covered all of the actions required of the lab. This tape recorder method also helps her maintain a record of what she has done. Of course, she saves the tapes, shares them with her colleagues, and uses them again with new groups of students.

Scaffolding Instruction

The teachers in the Respeto house all utilize scaffolding to support diverse learners. Scaffolding is the practice of following an instructional sequence to better aid learning. The following is a typical sequence (Wilkinson & Silliman, 2000) the teachers build into their lesson plans:

- Explicit modeling, usually in the form of a demonstration of a strategy or task
- Direct explanations of the strategy or task they have just shared, including the theoretical framework
- Eliciting student response by asking questions and probing for students' construction of meaning
- Verifying and clarifying through further questioning, so that any misinformation can be corrected

This practice echoes Vygotsky's (1978) theory of "zones of proximal development." Vygotsky theorized that when learners receive support just beyond what they can accomplish independently, they learn new skills and concepts.

The teachers of Respeto house have translated this pattern to Show, Tell, Question, and Clarify as a way to utilize scaffolding in the introduction of new material. A lesson in Ms. Caulfield's science class demonstrates this pattern. The class had been studying the spread of diseases in the Middle Ages, some of it due to poor hygiene and medical care. She set up a lab for students to examine common bacteria using microscopes. She began by showing the students what they would be doing using a video microscope hooked up to her computer and projected on a screen, thereby allowing all the students to view the prepared slides at 4×, 10×, and 40× powers. She then proceeded to tell them about the three objective lenses of the microscope. Next, she questioned students about the advantages and disadvantages of each lens power. Finally, she clarified some of the misinformation she heard, including Paul's suggestion that the 40× lens would be the best way to locate an object on a slide. She began the Show, Tell, Question, Clarify sequence again by demonstrating the difficulties of using the 40× lens for that purpose. Ms. Caulfield later commented that showing students first seemed to be more useful because students were able to ask higher order questions, because many of the procedural details had been demonstrated already.

Compacting

In compacting, students are assessed on their prior knowledge. Those students who already know the material are assigned other tasks, such as peer tutoring, library research, and math labs. This allows Mrs. Park, the social studies teacher, to focus her lesson on the students who really need it. Two rules guide her use of this strategy. First, the pre-assessment changes every week. One week it may be paper-pencil, the next could be small group, the next could be oral, and the following could include a performance. Second, all students must take the final assessment of the material, and their grade is based on that score.

One student, Julian, had "compacted out" because of his level of knowledge about medieval life. However, he had negotiated a contract to receive honors credit in this course. He spoke with Mrs. Park about his interest in the Middle Ages, and proposed translating his peers' projects into a website. He made an especially compelling case for doing so by comparing it to the role of the monks of the Middle Ages who created the beautiful illuminated manuscripts of the time.

Mrs. Park likes to offer compacting to her students because it has served two purposes. In addition to creating an in-class tutoring system, she has noticed that some of the students who were eligible for "compacting out" decided not to because they learned they did better on the tests when they participated in the lesson. Mrs. Park found this to be an effective way to engage some of her students.

Independent Projects

Mr. Amante, the English teacher, believes that work done outside of school should be interesting and should require students to work with at least one other person. He is most interested in independent projects (previously called homework) that require students to interact with their families. He is least interested in independent projects that encourage students to sit in their bedroom by themselves. Mr. Amante also likes independent projects that are challenging for students but not frustrating. This has led him to develop several projects, and not have all his students do the same project each night.

For this unit on the Middle Ages, some students interviewed their elder family members on how the role of children had changed during their lifetime. The unit had focused on the fact that children were not viewed as "children" in modern terms, but rather as little adults. They read informational texts about marriage laws of the time and were shocked to find out that girls married at twelve, and boys at fourteen! They compared their older family members' memories with those of the children of the Middle Ages. Mr. Amante found this independent project to be particularly successful for the ELL students because they could complete their assignment in their home language.

Other students worked together outside of school to film an I-Movie using the school's digital camera. (I-Movie software allows students to easily film and edit, and then add special effects and titles.) Inspired by their readings of *Catherine, Called Birdy* (Cushman, 1995) and *Matilda Bone* (Cushman, 2000), they created a "day in the life" comparison of a servant girl and the daughter of a lord. Jen, a student with a significant disability, used her Delta Talker augmentative communication device to perform her lines in the docudrama. Ms. Duong, the special education teacher, programmed the device in advance for Jen and her friends. Julian has plans to include this short I-Movie on the website.

Interest Groups

Chavez Middle School has an advisory period so that only half the students are at lunch at one time. The half who are not at lunch sign up for an advisory class based on the topics covered. For example, Ms. Duong, the special educator, has offered topics as diverse as The Titanic, 3-D Art, Horror Novels, and Careers in Human Services. These advisories are full of students interested in a specific topic and last for three weeks. At the end of the three weeks, students get to pick a new topic. Some students pick Ms. Duong regardless of what she is doing; others make different choices each term. Ms. Duong believes that these interest groups allow students to experience the richness of a curriculum and make choices about what they want to learn. She knows that the time she spends in advisory allows her to get to know students very well.

Concept Maps and Character Webs

Visual representations of complex ideas help students organize information. Developing concept or semantic maps is one strategy used by teachers because it provides insights about students' knowledge about the topic. Typically the main idea is placed in the center of the paper with a small circle drawn around it. Then lines are drawn from the circle to ideas that connect with the main idea. As you can imagine, there can be several sub-ideas to a main idea, and each sub-idea can have branches of ideas from it. For example, Ms. Caulfield's science class was studying the plague, also known as the Black Death, because of the black splotches on the victim's skin. They had examined the probable path of the disease, from its origins in Asia Minor around 1346 to its spread by *rattus rattus*, the common ship rat, along the major trade routes between East and West. They studied population charts and copies of primary source materials, such as census reports, and discovered that an estimated 25 million people died in the five years between 1347 and 1352. They had charted hygiene habits of the time (many people completely bathed only once, on their wedding day), food storage (salt was the major means of preserving meat), and medical treatments such as leeches and dunkings. One day she asked each student to take out a piece of paper and write inside a small circle the words "Black Death." The students were then asked to brainstorm lots of ideas that were connected to their main idea. Following this brainstorming, students were asked to transform their concept map into a three-paragraph paper. Ms. Caulfield's students will expand these concept maps again near the end of the unit, done in groups of four, as a way to review for the test. Not only can her students review information this way, but she can gain insights about areas that students may not understand.

Mr. Amante uses character webs to focus his students' thinking on people during his English class. He read aloud the chapter book *The Door in the Wall* (1989), a story about a young English boy who acquires a disability and is abandoned by the superstitious servants who were charged with caring for him. Each student was given a simple drawing of a person's head. As they learned more about Robin (the main character in the book), the students illustrated the simple drawing and placed key words around the head to describe him. Mr. Amante has found that the character webs help all of his students understand character development. He was especially pleased to find that students identified as having learning disabilities significantly improved their understanding of the story when they were required to create character webs. In addition to concept maps, Mr. Amante also uses clip art, illustrated vocabulary, videos, and computer websites to assist students in creating visual representations.

Writing Prompts and Questions

Mrs. Parks works with students to create a series of questions to answer as they read the social studies textbook and informational text. She has found that this helps focus their reading for specific information. This may be as simple as having students read the end-of-chapter questions prior to and throughout the reading of the chapter. (Many of the students thought this was "cheating" when she first suggested it! She assured them that it's what effective readers do.) Focusing on the questions helps students chunk, summarize, and synthesize the newly acquired information. When there are no end-of-unit questions, Mrs. Park and her students create questions that focus their reading. These questions are often first developed during the "what I want to learn" part of the KWL (Ogle, 1986, 1996) or by changing text subheadings into questions.

Students were divided into expert groups of six to read *How Would You Survive the Middle Ages?* (MacDonald, 1997), *Keeping Clean: Everyday History* (Stewart, 2000), *Life During the Middle Ages: The Way People Live* (Rice, 2000), or *Eyewitness: Medieval Life* (Langley, 2000). They searched for answers to the questions generated during the KWL, and then converted the questions and answers into a "Trivial Pursuit" game. As a culminating project, all the cards from the classes were combined for use in Ye Olde Medieval Trivial Pursuit Tournament. Their performance on the end-of-the unit test suggested to Mrs. Park that generating questions and answers was an effective study tool for her students.

During writing assignments, Mrs. Park has found that students perform better when she changes the questions into sentence starters. For example, instead of asking students to respond to a question like "What is the role of a vassal?" she rephrases it to read, "The role of a vassal is to . . ." Additional examples she developed include: "The economic effect of the Black Death was . . ." and "The Moors influence on European learning included . . ." This format for questioning is especially effective for her English language learners, who sometimes struggle with interrogatives in a new language, as well as her students with learning disabilities. Ms. Duong, the special education teacher, also provides clip art cut outs for Sonia and Tre, two students with significant disabilities, so that they can choose appropriate art to augment their dictated responses.

Tiered Assignments and Tests

Mr. Tabers, the mathematics teacher, has found that when students have choice in their assignments, they perform better. For this reason, he has a full page of assignments that students can do for his class. Each assignment is worth a maximum number of points, and students select which assignments to complete based on their interests. While other teachers have different rules regarding tiered assignments, Mr. Tabers lets his students do as many assignments as they want in order to earn the grade that they want in his class. For the Middle Schools Meets the Middle Ages unit, students could select a variety of medieval card games to research, construct, and then teach the class. These games included Piquet, a card game that relies on mental math; Noddy, an early version of cribbage that creates number sequences; or Byzantine chess, a tenth-century precursor of the modern game, played on a round board. Byzantine chess represents a more difficult mathematical challenge because students who choose this game must work in three-dimensional space.

In addition to the tiered assignments, Mr. Tabers uses tiered tests. His end-of-unit tests have five parts: true/false, multiple choice, short answer, short essay with illustration, and long essay. Mr. Tabers likes for his students to have experiences with different ways of demonstrating their knowledge so that they will do well on the statewide assessments. His use of tiered tests is unique. During test time, students are required to complete two sections of the test. When he returns the test the following day, he has graded the two sections that each student completed. The students then complete one more section of the test. He does this for several reasons. First, students can demonstrate their knowledge the best way they know how. Second, students learn to use the test as a tool. That is, there are answers to questions in other questions on a test. Third, students talk about the test during passing periods and lunch after the first administration. While the students think they are being sly, Mr. Tabers likes the fact that they are using their time to talk about the curriculum. Finally, he likes the idea that these tests communicate to students that knowledge is never complete, that there is always more to know and learn.

Accommodations and Modifications

Accommodations and modifications are techniques used by special educators to ensure that students with disabilities can access the core curriculum in general education classrooms (e.g., Castagnera, Fisher, Rodifer, & Sax, 1998). An *accommodation* is a change made to the teaching or testing procedures in order to provide a student with access to information and to create an equal opportunity to demonstrate knowledge and skills. Accommodations do not change the instructional level, content, or performance criteria for meeting the standards. Examples of accommodations include enlarging the print, Braille versions, providing oral versions of tests, and using calculators.

A *modification* is a change in what a student is expected to learn and/or demonstrate. While a student may be working on modified course content, the subject area remains the same as the rest of the class. If the decision is made to modify the curriculum, it is done in a variety of ways, for a variety of reasons, with a variety of outcomes. Again, modifications vary according to the situation. Listed below are four modification techniques:

* *Same—Only Less.* The assignment remains the same except the number of items are reduced. The items selected should be representative of the curriculum. For example, a social studies test that consisted of multiple choice questions each with five possible answers could be modified and the number of possible answers reduced to two.
* *Streamline the Curriculum.* The assignment is reduced in size, breadth, or focus to emphasize the key points. For example, in a language arts class, students may create an author study on Gary Paulsen with a reflective journal on themes and impressions of the books they read. A student with a disability may focus on identifying the themes of the books he or she reads, and then creating a display that uses pictures to support his or her writing on those main ideas.

- *Same Activity with Infused Objective.* The assignment remains the same but additional components such as IEP objectives or skills identified are incorporated. This is often done in conjunction with other accommodations and/or modifications to ensure that all IEP objectives are addressed. For example, if a student has an IEP objective to answer factual and inferential questions, the math teacher may need to remember to ask these types of questions so that the student can practice this skill in a natural setting.
- *Curriculum Overlapping.* The assignment in one area may be completed during another time. Some students work slowly and need more time to complete assignments while others need to explore the connections between various content areas. This strategy is especially helpful in these situations. For example, if a student participated in a poster project in his or her cooperative learning group during math centers, the product could also be used during language arts.

Deciding which technique to use depends on the type of assignment and the specific student. One assignment may only need to be reduced in size in order for the student to be successful, while another may incorporate infused objectives. Each of the techniques, as well as appropriate personal supports, should be considered for each situation. Keep in mind that *curriculum does not always need to be modified*—even when considering students with significant disabilities. When general education teachers provide multilevel instruction, changes to a lesson may not be necessary. Differentiating instruction allows all students a variety of ways to demonstrate knowledge while continuing to meet the requirements of the class. At other times, the curriculum can be made more accessible through accommodations and modifications. Figure 8.1 provides a list of additional curriculum accommodations and modifications.

Figure 8.1   Accommodations and Modifications Ideas

IDEAS FOR USE WITH INSTRUCTIONAL MATERIALS
- Provide a calculator
- Supply graph paper to assist in organizing and lining up math problems
- Tape lectures
- Allow film or video as supplements to or in place of text
- Provide practice opportunities using games, computers, language master, oral drills, and board work
- Offer a personal dry erase board
- Allow student to record thoughts and write while listening to audiotape or watching a video of the lecture or class assignment
- Provide visual aids to stimulate ideas
- Allow the use of computers for writing
- Provide student with ink stamps for numbers, letters, date, and signature
- Tape the assignment to the desk or provide a clipboard that can be clamped to the desk or wheelchair tray to secure papers
- Use print enlarger or light box to illuminate text
- Use tactile materials
- Find accompanying enrichment materials on the student's reading level
- Use adapted computer hardware or software

IDEAS FOR USE WITH IN-CLASS ACTIVITIES
- Break down new skills into small steps
- Simplify instruction by demonstrating and guiding learning one step at a time
- Role play historical events

- Underline or highlight important words and phrases
- Group students into pairs, threes, fours, etc. for different assignments and activities
- Pair students with different and complementary skills
- Pick from a book key words to read on each page
- Turn pages in book while others read
- Rewrite text or use easy to read versions
- Have student complete sentences supplied by the teacher orally or in writing
- Supply incomplete sentences for student to fill in appropriate words or phrases
- Engage students in read, write, pair, share activities
- Use hands-on activities
- Color code important words or phrases

IDEAS FOR USE WITH PROJECTS OR HOMEWORK
- Assign smaller quantities of work
- Relate problems to real-life situations
- Highlight problems to be completed
- Read problems and equations aloud
- Allow more time for completion
- Provide study questions in advance of an assignment
- Encourage oral contributions
- Assign concept maps
- Provide sample sentences for students to use as a model
- Dictate report to a partner who writes it out or types it on the computer
- Assign homework partners
- Assign group projects to illustrate a story setting (collages and dioramas)
- Substitute projects for written assignments and reports
- Use complementary software or adapted computer hardware
- Organize pictures instead of words into categories
- Have student survey other students using targeted questions on the topic

IDEAS FOR USE WITH ASSESSMENTS
- Underline or highlight text directions
- Read word problems aloud
- Reword problems using simpler language
- Underline key words
- Space problems farther apart on the page
- Reduce the number of questions by selecting representative items
- Permit oral responses
- Put choices for answers on index cards
- Use the sentence or paragraph as a unit of composition rather than an essay
- Allow oral responses to tests using a tape recorder
- Use photographs in oral presentations to the class
- Reword test questions in easier terms
- Assign final group projects with each student responsible for specific roles
- Encourage the use of other media for final products (film, video, audio, photos, drawings, performances,

Conclusions

As you can tell, many of the supports that diverse learners require can be provided as part of the instructional arrangements in the general education classroom. Several years of research suggests that these instructional strategies are beneficial for all students, not only those identified as gifted, English language learners, or those with disabilities. Taken together, curriculum and instructional supports address many of the support needs for diverse learners.

Section Three

Completed Lesson Plan by Jeff Simon

Estuarine Ecosystems Unit Objectives

Estuary Ecosystems Unit Planner

Estuary Report Writing Worksheet

The A+ Guide to Estuary Ecosystems!

Model Estuary Demonstration Teacher Notes

*Comparing the Salinity of Tap, River, Estuary, and Sea Waters
   Teacher Notes*

Introducing: Estuaries!

*Creating a Word Processing Document at Monroe Clark
   Middle School*

Dead Duck! Teacher Notes

The San Elijo Lagoon/Estuary Investigation

Habits in an Estuary Ecosystem

Formatting and Turning in Your Estuary Report

Spell Checking and Printing Your Estuary Report

Ecology Pre/post Test

*A Vision for the Future … Giving San Diego's Estuaries
   to the People*

ESTUARINE ECOSYSTEMS
UNIT OBJECTIVES

I. SCIENCE

To develop a conceptual understanding of the following science content standards and scientific concepts, particularly as they relate to estuarine ecosystems:

San Diego City Schools Science Content Standards

7.4.a.	Plants have structures that contribute to their ability to survive in their environment.
7.4.b.	Animals have structures that contribute to their ability to survive in their particular environments.
7.6.b.	Matter is transferred from one organism to another, repeatedly, and between organisms and their physical environment. Almost all food energy comes originally from sunlight.
7.6.c.	Organisms have particular roles in ecosystems, and interact in a variety of ways.
7.8.a.	As water passes through the water cycle, it dissolves minerals and carries them to the oceans.
7.11.a.	Science investigations are one way to learn about the world.
7.12.a-d.	The following unifying concepts prove fruitful in explanation, theory, and observation: models, consistency and change, systems, and form and function.
7.13.a.	Technology and human activities have an impact on environmental quality.

Key Concepts

coastal plain	habitat	food web
estuary	shelter	food chain
tides	population	cycle
salinity	organism	energy
brackish	threat	decomposer
		producer
		consumer
		adaptation

II. COMPUTER LITERACY

To type, format, spell-check, and submit a word-processing document by following instructional handouts.

San Diego City Schools Technology Performance Standard

7.3b.2.	The student uses word-processing applications to produce project reports.

III. READING

To understand, analyze, synthesize, and evaluate informational text and functional documents, connecting text with prior knowledge and experience.

San Diego City Schools Language Arts Performance Standards: Reading

7.4.1.   The student reads informational materials to develop understanding and expertise and produces written work that:
  • Makes and supports reasonable conclusions and opinions about the texts read.
  • Restates or summarizes information.
  • Extends ideas.
  • Makes connections between new information, prior knowledge, and related topics.
  • Supports arguments with data.

7.4.3.   The student demonstrates familiarity with a variety of functional documents (documents written to assure that a specific task is accomplished) and produces written work that:
  • Identifies the sequence of activities needed to carry out a procedure.

IV. WRITING

To effectively write a report about estuarine ecosystems in which the student a) demonstrates an ability to read and understand informational text, and b) represents and explains the scientific concepts listed above. In doing so, the student follows the conventions of standard, written language, and uses steps of the writing process as needed.

San Diego City Schools Language Arts Performance Standards: Writing

7.6.4.   The student produces a report, e.g., in science, in which the writer:
  • Provides an interesting beginning that sets a context for a topic.
  • Develops a controlling idea and a theme that conveys a perspective on the subject.
  • Creates an organizing structure appropriate to purpose, audience, and context.
  • Includes appropriate facts and details.
  • Attempts to exclude inappropriate information.
  • Uses a range of strategies appropriate to the type of report, such as providing facts and details, comparing and contrasting, and describing.
  • Provides a sense of closure to the writing.

ESTUARY ECOSYSTEMS UNIT PLANNER

Lesson	Essential Questions	Activities	Resources
1	• What do you already know about estuaries, ecosystems, habitats, and food webs? • What more would you like to know aoout estuaries, ecosystems, habitats, and food webs? • What will be expected of you during this unit on ecosystems?	Estuary Ecosystems K-W(-L)	"Estuary Report Writing Worksheet" (student handout) "The A+ Guide to Estuary Ecosystems" (student handout – project overview)
2	• What is an estuary, where are estuaries located, and how are they created? • What are tides and how do they affect estuaries? • Qualitatively, what is the salinity of estuary water compared to river water and ocean water?	Making a Model Estuary	"Model Estuary Demonstration" (teacher notes)
3	• Quantitatively, what is the salinity of estuary water compared to river water, ocean water, and tap water?	Lab: Comparing the Salinity of Four Water Types	"Comparing the Salinity of Tap, River, Estuary, and Sea Waters" (student handout – lab)
4	• How do you take Cornell-style notes and write a paragraph to show that you understand something that you've read? • What is an estuary, where are some lccal estuaries, and how are estuaries formed? • What kind of water is found in an estuary and how does it change? • What are the benefits and challenges for organisms that live in estuaries?	Reading & Note-taking: "Introducing: Estuaries!" Report Writing: "Estuary Basics"	"Introducing Estuaries!" (student handout – informational text) "The A+ Guide to Estuary Ecosystems" (student handout – project overview)
5	• How do you open, create, and save a report on a computer at Monroe Clark Middle School?	Word Processing – I	"Creating a Word Processing Document at Monroe Clark Middle School" (student handout – instructions)

ESTUARY ECOSYSTEMS UNIT PLANNER—continued

Lesson	Essential Questions	Activities	Resources
6	• What is a habitat? • How are populations of organisms affected by their habitats? • How can you make a graph that shows how a population of organisms changes over time?	Dead Duck!	"Dead Duck!" (teacher notes)
7	• What can you learn about estuaries, ecosystems, habitat, and food webs from a visit to a local estuary?	Estuary Field Trip	"San Elijo Lagoon/ Estuary Experience" with map (student handouts)
8	• What is a habitat, and what habitats can be found in a local estuary? • What are some threats to the habitats in a local estuary? • What are some solutions that could help protect our local estuaries?	Reading & Note-taking: "Habitats in an Estuary Ecosystem" Report Writing: "Habitats in a Local Estuary"	"Habitats in an Estuary Ecosystem" (student handout – informational text) "The A+ Guide to Estuary Ecosystems" (student handout – project overview)
9	• How do your format a report on a computer at Monroe Clark Middle School?	Word Processing – II	"Formatting Your Estuary Report" (student handout – instructions)
10	• How are matter and energy transferred between organisms in an estuary ecosystem? • How can you make and read a food web?	Estuary Food Web Posters	"Making an Estuarine Food Web" (student handout – images)
11	• What are some alternative opinions held towards the environment?	Mach presentation: "A Vision for the Future"	"A Vision for the Future" (mach presentation notes)
12	• How do you write a conclusion to a report?	Report Writing: "Conclusion"	"The A+ Guide to Estuary Ecosystems" (student handout – project overview)

Lesson	Essential Questions	Activities	Resources
13	• How do you write an introduction to a report?	Report Writing: "Introduction"	"The A+ Guide to Estuary Ecosystems" (student handout – project overview)
14	• How do you check your spelling and print a report on a computer at Monroe Clark Middle School?	Word Processing – III	"Spell-checking and Printing Your Estuary Report" (student handout)
15	• What did you learn from this unit about estuaries, ecosystems, habitats, and food webs?	Test	"Ecosystems Post Test" (student handout)
Ext.	• How can biologists better understand the interdependency amongst organisms in an ecosystem?	Owl Pellet Dissection	"Rodent Stick Sheet" (student handout)

ESTUARY REPORT
WRITING WORKSHEET

Name _____

Date _____   Period _____

What I already KNEW about estuary . . .	What I WANTED TO KNOW about estuary . . .	What I LEARNED about estuary . . .
Environment:	Environment:	Environment:
Habitat:	Habitat:	Habitat:
Organisms:	Organisms:	Organisms:

Name _____

Date _____ Period _____

Mr. Simon's Science City

The A+ Guide to Estuary Ecosystems!

at Monroe Clark Middle School

PART I—ESTUARY REPORT

You will write a report about estuary ecosystems. Your report should be two or three pages and must be typed, formatted, and spell-checked on the computers here at school. You will learn about estuary ecosystems by reading two different sources of information. While reading, you will take Cornell-style notes in your own words. You will then use your notes to write a report that includes the following sections and answers the following questions:

INTRODUCTION
- Before you did this report, what did you already know about the environment, habitats, and organisms found in estuaries, and what more did you want to learn?
- What information did you read to learn more about these topics?
- How will your report be organized?

ESTUARY ENVIRONMENT
- What is an estuary, where are some local estuaries, and how are estuaries formed?
- What kind of water is found in an estuary and how does it change?
- What are the benefits and challenges for organisms that live in estuaries?

HABITATS IN A LOCAL ESTUARY
- What are habitats, and what habitats can be found in a local estuary?
- What are some threats to the habitats in a local estuary?
- What are some solutions that could help protect our local estuaries?

CONCLUSION
- What do you think should be the future of our local estuaries?
- How are the organisms, habitats, and environment related to each other in an estuary ecosystem?

PART II—STUDY GUIDE

By the end of this unit, you should understand the following concepts, be able to answer the following questions, and be prepared to demonstrate your knowledge on a multiple choice test:

Vocabulary/Important Concepts

Ecosystem

estuary	habitat	food web
tides	shelter	food chain
salinity	population	cycle
brackish	organism	energy
	threat	decomposer
		producer
		consumer
		adaptation

Essential Questions

1. What is an estuary, where are estuaries located, and how are they created?

2. What are tides and how do they affect estuaries?

3. What is the salinity of estuary water compared to river water and ocean water?

4. What is a habitat?

5. How are populations of organisms affected by their habitats?

6. How do plants and animals adapt to their environments?

7. How are matter and energy transferred between organisms in an estuary ecosystem?

8. How can you make and read a food web?

MODEL ESTUARY DEMONSTRATION
TEACHER NOTES

Science Objectives

To develop a conceptual understanding of the following essential questions, science content standards, key concepts particularly as they relate to estuarine ecosystems:

Essential Questions
- What is an estuary, where are estuaries located, and how are they created?
- What are tides and how do they affect estuaries?
- Qualitatively, what is the salinity of estuary water compared to river water and ocean water?

San Diego City Schools Science Content Standards
7.8.a.	As water passes through the water cycle, it dissolves minerals and carries them to the oceans.
7.11.a.	Science investigations are one way to learn about the world.
7.12.a-d.	The following unifying concepts prove fruitful in explanation, theory, and observation: models, consistency and change, and systems.

Key Concepts

coastal plain estuary	salinity
tides	brackish

Materials
*(Note: * indicates materials that can be found in the FOSS Kit: Landforms module)*

stream table*	stream table support*
river sand/pumice mixture*	plastic cup with hole*
ruler*	duct tape

Set-up

Procedure

1. Derive students' background knowledge regarding the essential questions for this lesson.

2. Present students with an overview of the answers to the essential questions, taking into consideration their background knowledge.

3. Inform students that they are about to witness a model estuary being formed. Invite them to gather around a table in the center of the room upon which the equipment is set up.

4. With the cup empty, elicit a description of the setting from the students including the following features: coast, cliff, slope, rainwater, and ocean basin. Ask them to predict what they think will happen when the cup is filled with water; allow for any speculation.

5. Fill the cup with water and point out the following features as they occur: erosion, river valley, floodplain, delta, fresh water, ocean, salt, and salt water.

6. Point out that this is not yet the whole story of an estuary's formation. Elicit from students the fact that the tides must somehow be simulated. Slowly begin to raise and lower the end of the stream table so that the salty ocean water gently but repetitively floods the model river valley.

7. Elicit from students the following features: where the estuary is located, how the shape of the estuary is affected by the tides, and how the tides affect the salinity of the estuary water.

COMPARING THE SALINITY OF TAP, RIVER, ESTUARY, AND SEA WATERS
TEACHER NOTES

Science Objectives

To develop a conceptual understanding of the following essential questions, science content standards, key concepts particularly as they relate to estuarine ecosystems:

Essential Question
• What is the salinity of estuary water compared to river water, ocean water, and tap water?

San Diego City Schools Science Content Standards

7.8.a.	As water passes through the water cycle, it dissolves minerals and carries them to the oceans (and leaves them behind when it evaporates).
7.11.a.	Science investigations are one way to learn about the world.
7.12.a-d.	The following unifying concepts prove fruitful in explanation, theory, and observation: models, consistency and change, and systems.

Key Concepts

water cycle	precipitation	evaporation
salinity	condensation	brackish

Materials (per lab group)

ring stand	flint sparker	ring clamp
100 ml beaker	wire gauze	goggles
Bunsen burner	safety glove	rubber tubing
balance	water sample	
	(tap, ocean, river, or estuary)	

Set-up

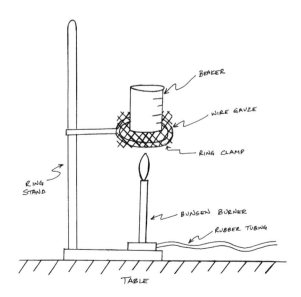

Procedure

1. Derive students' background knowledge regarding the essential question for this lesson by eliciting their hypothesis of the order of the four water types from lowest salinity to highest salinity.

2. Instruct students to begin preparing a lab report that begins with the title of the experiment, the essential question, and their hypothesis.

3. Elicit possible procedures from students as to how they could measure, quantitatively, the amount of salt in each of the four water samples, drawing their attention to the lab equipment as a cue.

4. Review the proper lab procedure for evaporation of liquids, including necessary measurements, safety precautions, and directions. In their lab groups, instruct students to outline the experimental procedure that will be conducted. Instruct them to include a section with safety precautions.

5. Instruct students to create a data table in which they will have entry spaces available for measurements of the mass of an empty beaker and a beaker with salt, the calculated mass of the salt, the average mass of the salt, and the percent difference of their findings from the average.

6. Reinforce the behavioral expectations for this activity. Allow students thirty minutes to conduct the experiment in which they evaporate 20 ml of a single water sample, including measurements, procedures, and clean up.

7. Have students enter the final mass of the salt in their water sample in a master data table on the overhead projector. Together, calculate the average masses of salt of each type of water. Instruct students to calculate their percent differences from the averages.

8. Discuss conclusions and analyze possible sources of error. Instruct students to write their conclusions and error analyses to complete their lab reports.

INTRODUCING: ESTUARIES!

An estuary is a body of water formed when fresh water from rivers and streams flows into the ocean and mixes with the salty seawater. Estuaries and the areas around them are places of change from land to sea, and from fresh to salt water. Although the ocean's tides affect estuaries, the areas are protected from the full force of ocean waves by cliffs, mud, or sand that separate the estuary from the sea. This, along with a constant supply of nutrients from rivers, makes estuaries incredibly rich places for plants, animals, and other organisms.

Estuaries come in all shapes and sizes and are located along the coasts of every continent in the world except for Antarctica. Some examples of local estuaries include the Tijuana River Estuary near the U.S.-Mexican border, the San Dieguito River Valley near the Del Mar Fairgrounds, and San Elijo Lagoon in North County San Diego. There are four different types of estuaries: coastal plain estuaries, fjords, tectonic estuaries, and bar-built estuaries. All of the estuaries near San Diego are coastal plain estuaries. Coastal plain estuaries occur because the water level of the ocean rises each day, flooding river valleys with seawater.

The salinity and water level within an estuary constantly change, making it a very harsh, dynamic place for plants and animals to live. Most of the time, and in most parts of an estuary, fresh water from rivers mixes with salt water from the ocean to create *brackish* water. Brackish water is less salty than ocean water, but more salty than fresh water. The salinity of this brackish water, however, does not always stay the same. The water level and the amount of salt in the water constantly change depending on the level of the ocean water, and the amount of rain. When there is a lot of rain or when the sea level is high, most of the land in an estuary gets flooded with water. During a dry summer, or at low tide, the water in an estuary is lost to the ocean and mud flats are all that remain.

Most plants and animals live either on land *or* in water, and if they live in the water, they live either in salt water *or* fresh water, not both. On one hand, estuaries are difficult places for organisms to live because the water level and salinity are constantly changing. The plants and animals in an estuary, however, have adapted to their environment over millions of years to be able to deal with this harsh situation. On the other hand, estuaries are a perfect place for a variety of living things to survive since rivers act as a constant source of life for estuaries. Rivers carry dead plants and other *organic material* into the estuaries, and that plays an important role in making a healthy ecosystem. The nutrients that the rivers bring create rich soil that allows plants to grow strong and quickly, providing habitats for animals. The material carried by the river also provides food for bacteria, which play an important role in the many food webs in an estuary that include thousands of species of animals like insects, worms, snails, crabs, fish, ducks, birds, and mammals.

CREATING A WORD PROCESSING DOCUMENT
AT MONROE CLARK MIDDLE SCHOOL

1. If the computer isn't already on, push the start button with the triangle on it located in the top right corner of the *keyboard* (if that doesn't work, turn it on using the switch on the back of the computer).

2. In the "**Name:**" box, enter your name, last name first, exactly as it appears on the Monroe Clark computer ID card, then press the tab button located on the left side of the keyboard. Enter your password in the "**Password:**" box, and press **return**.

3. In the <u>dialogue box</u> that appears, double click on "**Science City.**"

4. In the <u>window</u> that appears, double click the "**Items for Science City**" icon.

5. In the window that appears, double click the "**Microsoft Word**" icon.

6. *Before you start typing, save your new document in a file in your personal folder!*

   A. Go to the "**file**" menu located on the *toolbar* and choose "**save as…**"

   B. In the *dialogue box* that appears, click the button that says "**New Folder.**"

   C. In the *dialogue box* that appears, type "**science**" and press **return**

   D. In the box that says "**Save Current Document As**" type "YOUR NAME's Estuary Report" and press **return**

   E. At the top of the *toolbar*, it should now say YOUR NAME's Estuary Report

(Remember that the underlined terms are computer terms that you are expected to know!)

DEAD DUCK!
TEACHER NOTES

Science Objectives

To develop a conceptual understanding of the following essential questions, science content standards, key concepts particularly as they relate to estuarine ecosystems:

Essential Questions
• What is habitat?
• How are populations of organisms affected by their habitats?
• How can you make a graph that shows how a population of organisms changes over time?

San Diego City Schools Science Content Standards

7.6.b.   Matter is transferred from one organism to another, repeatedly, and between organisms and their physical environment. Almost all food energy comes originally from sunlight.

7.11.a.   Science investigations are one way to learn about the world.

7.12.a-d.   The following unifying concepts prove fruitful in explanation, theory, and observation: models, consistency and change, and systems.

Key Concepts

habitat   shelter   population

Materials/Set-up

bullhorn
open space (e.g., courtyard or field)

Procedure

1. Derive students' background knowledge regarding habitat—its components and its role in an ecosystem.

2. Explain to students that habitat, in fact, includes four components: food, water, shelter, and space, and that in this human model they will witness how an animal's population might change as the availability of these components fluctuates.

3. Number students 1-2-3-4-5, 1-2-3-4-5, etc. until all students have been assigned a number.

4. Review the behavioral expectations for this activity. Instruct students with the number one that they are ducks and should line up on one side of the area. Instruct all other students to line up on the other side of the area. Both lines should be facing each other (as in the game "Red Rover").

5. Using the bullhorn, explain the rules of play:

    a. All students turn around.

    b. Students numbered 2, 3, 4, or 5 represent various components of habitat, so they make a sign to represent which component they choose to be in the first round:

food	=	both hands on belly
water	=	both hands on mouth
shelter	=	both hands over head making a "roof"
space	=	both arms open wide

    c. Students numbered 1 represent ducks that are seeking various components of their habitat. Accordingly, they each make a sign to represent one component that they feel the need to seek in the first round.

    d. On the count of three, all students turn around, holding their signs. The ducks then run across the area and touch one of the components of habitat that provides their need. Together, they return to the "duck" side of the area.

    e. The teacher records the resulting number of ducks in a prepared data table on an overhead transparency.

    f. This process is repeated fifteen times. Each time the students are permitted to change their component of habitat that they represent or need. When a duck cannot locate his/her sought-after component, he/she becomes a "Dead Duck!" and, appropriately for an ecosystem, transforms into habitat.

6. Upon returning to class, instruct students to create a line graph of the duck population versus years (corresponding to the rounds).

7. Guide students through a discussion regarding how the duck population was affected by its habitat.

THE SAN ELIJO LAGOON/ESTUARY INVESTIGATION

INSTRUCTIONS: Find examples of the items listed below and show their locations on your map using the symbols that are given. In addition, write a description of items with white numbers (À, Á, Â), and draw pictures of items with black numbers (¶, ·, ‚).

NON-LIVING FACTORS

___ The place where the ocean water enters the estuary (▲)

___ Roads (——), freeways (══), train tracks (▦), & trails (········) that block the water

　　① – Explain how these threaten the estuary's habitats.

___ Bridges that let the water move under them (IIII)

___ The ocean (⋀⋀)

___ Houses that are built near the estuary (⌂)

　　② – Explain how these threaten the estuary's habitats.

___ Water Pollution Control Facility (⊗)

　　③ – Explain how this effects the estuary's habitats.

___ Trash (⊖) ❶

___ An area that's very sandy (⸬⸬)

___ A long shady tunnel (○ ○ ○) ④ – How do you think this tunnel was created?

HABITAT

___ Salt marsh (""""""") ⑤ – Describe how it looks.

___ Mud flats (+++++) ⑥ – Describe how they look.

___ Fresh and brackish water marsh (||||||||) ⑦ – Describe how it looks.

___ Brackish water river (>>>>>) ⑧ – Describe how it looks.

___ Upland area (^^^^^^) ⑨ – Describe how it looks.

___ Strong smelling plants (♣)

___ Purple flowers (✳)　　___ Pickleweed (⊛)　　___ Seaweed (✧)

___ Yellow flowers (✿)　　___ Cattails (Y) ❸　　___ Algae (◉)

___ Orange flowers (✸)　　___ Cactus (✳)　　___ Ice plant (❀)

FOOD WEBS / WILDLIFE

___ Bones from a dead seal (☠)

___ Lizard (✛) ⑩ – What was it doing, and why was it doing that?

___ Fish (✪) ⑪ – What was it doing, and why was it doing that?

___ An insect (♠) ❹

___ Animal poop (∝)

___ Snake (〰)

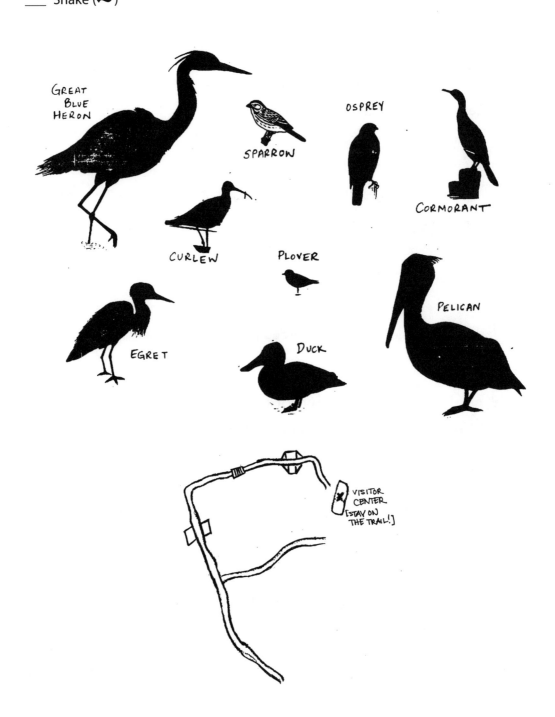

HABITATS IN AN ESTUARY ECOSYSTEM

A habitat is a place where an organism can successfully live. An animal's habitat includes sources of food, water, shelter, space, and all of its other needs. For example, the great blue heron is a common bird found in an estuary. Its habitat includes the rivers, mud flats, and marshes of the estuary where it wades through the water hunting for fish, catching them with its long bill.

The different habitats in an estuary include salt marsh, mudflats, brackish water rivers, fresh and brackish water marsh, and upland areas. The *salt marsh* habitat consists mostly of plants like salt grass and pickleweed. These plants have special adaptations so that they can handle being covered in salt water when the water level in an estuary is high. Salt grass, for example, gets rid of extra salt by pushing it out onto the surface of its leaves, so it looks like it's covered with little diamonds sparkling in the sun. When the level of the water in an estuary is low, the *mudflat* habitat can be seen. Mudflats don't look like they are home to very many organisms, but really they're filled with tons of worms, snails, and bacteria. *Brackish water rivers* are home to most of the fish and ducks in an estuary. These rivers flow in one direction when the tide rises, and they flow in the opposite direction when the level of the ocean water goes down. Sometimes seaweed floats in the brackish water rivers or gets dropped by the river onto the mudflats. This seaweed provides shelter and food for small organisms. *Fresh and brackish water marsh* is often filled with tall marsh plants like cattails and bulrush. Both plants have leaves that look like tall spears that stick out of the water. Birds and animals use them to hide in and to make nests from. Finally, *upland areas* are the dry lands above the water level of the estuary. The ocean doesn't affect these parts of an estuary. Upland areas are filled with taller trees and bushes that provide shelter and food for lots of animals, including insects, lizards, rabbits, and snakes. Freshwater streams often run through the upland areas providing a source of water for plants and animals.

All of these habitats in an estuary are fragile, and they are often in danger of being destroyed. Three examples of threats to estuary ecosystems are pollution, blocking the opening between an estuary and the ocean, and invasion by strange plants. Trash isn't the only kind of pollution that can litter the habitats in an estuary. In fact, most of the pollution in an estuary can't be seen! For example, fertilizers and pesticides often flow into estuaries in streams after they pass through farms. Also, pollutants from cars often get washed off the streets into pipes that drain into estuaries. A different problem happens when people build roads, freeways, and railroad tracks across an estuary. This blocks the natural flow of the water in and out of the estuary. When the water in an estuary stays still for too long, a lot of algae grows. As a result, large amounts of bacteria develop which use up all of the oxygen for fish and other organisms to breathe. This reduces the food supplies for birds and other animals. Last, people have brought many types of plants from other countries that grow near estuaries. These foreign plants sometimes grow faster than the plants that were already growing there, and they destroy a lot of the habitat. For example, in Southern California, ice plant is used along free-ways and hillsides, but it has started growing very quickly in natural places like estuaries. The ice plant grows especially in the upland areas and kills a lot of the plants that animals use for food and shelter. All of these problems threaten the habitats in estuaries and all of the organisms that depend on them.

FORMATTING AND TURNING IN YOUR ESTUARY REPORT

1. Open your "Estuary Report" by following these steps:

   A. Turn on the computer.

   B. Enter your user name and password.

   C. In the dialogue *box* that appears, *double click* on "**Science City**."

   D. In the window that appears, double click on your ***personal folder*** (the folder with your name, <u>not</u> "Items for Science City").

   E. In the window that appears, double click on the "**Science**" folder.

   F. In the window that appears, double click the "**YOUR NAME's Estuary Report**" icon.

2. *Highlight* your name, date, and period:

   A. Move the *cursor* to the top left corner of the screen, before your name.

   B. Push the *mouse-button* and hold it.

   C. *Drag* the cursor down and to the right until your name, date, and period are highlighted.

3. Set your name, date, and period to the right by clicking the "align right" button.

4. Format your title:

   A. Highlight the words "Title Goes Here."

   B. Click the "center" button (see below).

   C. Go to the "**Size**" menu and choose "18 Point".

5. Format your text:

   A. Highlight ALL of the words in the paragraphs that you have written.

   B. Click the "justify" button (see below).

   C. Click the "increase line space" button <u>twice</u> so that your report is double-spaced (see below).

6. Do not make any more changes to the font, size, or style of your work!

7. Warning: If you make a mistake and lose all of your work, get a teacher and wait—
   don't click anything!

8. Continue typing your report. Remember, every five minutes, go to the "**File**" menu
   and choose "**Save**" (<u>NOT</u> "Save As...").

9. When it's time to stop working:

   A. Go to the "**File**" menu and choose "**Quit**."

   B. If a dialogue box appears, press **return** to save your work.

   C. Go to the "**File**" menu and choose "**Duplicate**."

   D. Move the "**Science**" window by clicking the top of it and moving it with your
       mouse so that you can see the "**Items for YOUR NAME**" window with the "**Hand
       in f**" folder in it.

   E. Drag "**YOUR NAME's Estuary Report Copy**" to the folder that says "**Hand in f**" and
       press **return** when the **!** dialogue box appears.

   F. Go to the "**File**" menu and choose "**Go to At Ease...**"

SPELL CHECKING AND PRINTING YOUR ESTUARY REPORT

1. Log-on to the computer and open your "Estuary Report" as usual.

2. Finish typing your report.

3. Check your spelling:

    A. Put the cursor in the top left corner, to the left of your name.

    B. Go to the "**Edit**" menu and choose "**Writing Tools**" then "**Check Document Spelling...**"

    C. A dialogue box will appear. You can move it around to see your text by clicking the top of the box and moving it with your mouse.

    D. If a word is not spelled correctly, find the correct word in the list of suggestions and double-click on it; the computer will then fix it.

    E. If the computer says that a word is not spelled correctly, but you know that it is correct (like your name), click on **Skip**.

    F. In the dialogue box that appears when the computer is done correcting the spelling, click on **Done**.

3. Print your work:

    A. Go to the "**File**" menu and choose "**Print...**".

    B. In the dialogue box that appears, click on "**Print**".

    C. *Do Not Go To The Printer—This Will Disturb the Class!*

Your teacher will get your report from the printer at the end of the period.

ECOLOGY PRE/POST TEST

1. Which type of water has the highest salinity?
   a. brackish water from an estuary
   b. fresh water from a river
   c. tap water from a sink
   d. salt water from the ocean

2. Estuaries form _____ .
   a. where rivers end at the ocean
   b. where there are a large variety of plants
   c. where there are a large variety of animals
   d. where there are mud flats

Use the bird pictures below to answer questions 3 & 4:

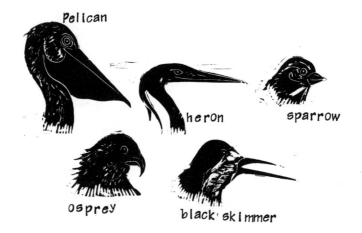

3. Which birds' beak is best adapted to crush seeds?
   a. pelican
   b. heron
   c. sparrow
   d. osprey
   e. black skimmer

4. All of these birds compete for the same food **except** for the _____ .
   a. pelican
   b. heron
   c. sparrow
   d. black skimmer

5. Which of these adaptations does not help a heron hunt for fish?
   a. long legs
   b. a long neck
   c. a long beak
   d. long feathers

Use the graph below to answer questions 6 & 7.

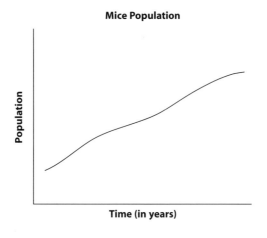

6. What information does the graph provide?
   a. how many years have passed
   b. how the mice population has changed with time
   c. how the mice population changes

7. According to the graph, what is happening to the population size over time?
   a. population size increases over time
   b. population size decreases over time
   c. population size remains the same

Use the following graph for questions 8–10.

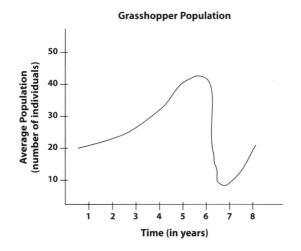

8. What is the average number of organisms in the population at year 1?
   a. 10
   b. 20
   c. 30
   d. 40
   e. 50

9. What happens to the average population between the years 1 and 5?
   a. it increases
   b. it decreases
   c. it remains the same
   d. none of the above

10. When does it look like there was a natural disaster, like maybe a fire?
    a. 2
    b. 4
    c. 6
    d. 8
    e. none of the above

Use the diagram below to answer questions 11–15.

11. According to the diagram, shrubs are _____ .
    a. decomposers
    b. producers
    c. second-order consumers
    d. first-order consumers

12. What is the main source of energy for all living things?
    a. sun
    b. water
    c. air
    d. wind

13. This diagram is an example of a _____ ?
    a. food line
    b. food web
    c. food chain
    d. food group

14. Which one does not get eaten by another animal?
    a. snake
    b. deer
    c. hawk
    d. grasses

15. Which of these shows a correct food chain for this web?
    a. shrubs ⟶ insects ⟶ snakes ⟶ hawk
    b. shrubs ⟶ rabbit ⟶ shrew ⟶ lion
    c. shrubs ⟶ squirrel ⟶ snakes ⟶ hawk
    d. shrubs ⟶ deer ⟶ lion

16. corn ⟶ mouse ⟶ owl ⟶ snake
    Which animal in this food chain usually eats plants?
    a. owl
    b. grass
    c. mouse
    d. snake

Use the diagram to answer questions 17–19.

17. Which animal eats the mouse?
    a. rabbit
    b. grass
    c. grasshopper
    d. owl
    e. small bird

18. Which is the prey for the small bird?
    a. rabbit
    b. grass
    c. grasshopper
    d. owl
    e. eagle

19. Which does not get eaten by anything?
    a. snake
    b. rabbit
    c. owl
    d. small bird
    e. eagle

20. This food web shows _____ .
    a. all the animals that live together
    b. the animals that interact
    c. the direction energy flows
    d. who is in charge

21. Which would probably cause a decrease in the rabbit population?
    a. a decrease in mice
    b. a decrease in foxes
    c. an increase in grasshoppers
    d. an increase in hawks

earthworm
eats soil

caterpillar
eats leaves

shrew
eats salamanders, snails and
centipedes

owl
eats rodents and birds

slug
eats leaves

centipede
eats beetle larvae and
caterpillars

deer mouse
eats Plants

beetle larva
eats soil

vole
eats Plants

weasel
eats shrew, mole, and deer mouse

rat
eats plants

house mouse
eats Plants

salamander
eats slugs, caterpillars
and beetle larvae

snail
eats leaves

song bird

eats worms,
beetle larvae,
caterpillars
and seeds

mole
eats slugs and earthworms

Plants   leaves   seeds   soil

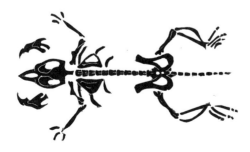

A Vision for the Future ...
Giving San Diego's
Estuaries to the People

Bill Hadley
Land for People Coalition

- Population of San Diego will Double by 2010!

- Cities Are Overcrowded!

- Local Estuaries Are in High Population Density Zones (HPDs)
  — We Need More Space!!!

- Environmentalists Create FALSE Image of Estuaries!

- Estuary Animal Facts:
  — Very Few Species
  — Not Interdependent
  — Adaptable

- Estuary Animal Facts:
  — Very Few Livable Areas
  — Unnecessary for Animals
  — Adaptable

- Basic Estuary Facts:
  — Shallow, Salty, Muddy
  — Not Suitable for Organisms
  — Very Recent Formations

REFERENCES

Alexander, P. A., & Jetton, T. L. (2000). Learning from text: A multidimensional and developmental perspective. In M. L. Kamil, P. B. Mosenthal, P. D. Pearson, & R. Barr (Eds.) *Handbook of reading research: Volume III* (pp. 285–310). Mahwah, NJ: Lawrence Erlbaum.

Allen, J., & Gonzalez, K. (1998). *There's room for me here: Literacy workshop in the middle school.* York, ME: Stenhouse.

Almasi, J. F. (1995). The nature of fourth graders' sociocognitive conflicts in peer-led and teacher-led discussions of literature. *Reading Research Quarterly, 30,* 314–351.

Alvarez, M. C. (1998). Developing critical and imaginative thinking within electronic literacy. *NASSP Bulletin, 82*(600), 41–47.

Alvermann, D. E. (1991). The discussion web: A graphic aid for learning across the curriculum. *The Reading Teacher, 45,* 92–99.

Alvermann, D. E., & Hagood, M. C. (2000). Fandom and critical media literacy. *Journal of Adolescent & Adult Literacy, 43,* 436–446.

Amer, A. A. (1997). The effect of the teacher's reading aloud on the reading comprehension of ESL students. *ELT Journal 1997, 51*(1), 43–47.

Ames, R., & Ames, C. (Eds.). (1984). *Motivation in education: Student motivation* (Vol. 1). New York: Academic Press.

Anders, P. L., & Bos, C. S. (1986). Semantic feature analysis: An interactive strategy for vocabulary development and text comprehension. *Journal of Reading, 29,* 610–616.

Andrews, S. E. (1997). Writing to learn in content area reading class. *Journal of Adolescent & Adult Literacy, 41,* 141–142.

Asher, J. J. (1996). *Learning another language through actions* (5th Ed.). Los Gatos, CA: Sky Oaks Productions.

Atwell, N. (1998). *In the middle: New understandings about writing, reading, and learning.* (2nd Ed.) Portsmouth, NH: Boynton/Cook.

August, D., & Hakuta, K. (Eds.). (1998). *Educating language-minority children.* Washington, DC: National Academy Press.

Ausubel, D. P. (1978). In defense of advance organizers: A reply to the critics. *Review of Educational Research, 48,* 251–257.

Baines, L. (1998). The future of the written word. In J. S. Simmons & L. Baines (Eds.), *Language study in middle school, high school, and beyond* (pp. 190–214). Newark, DE: International Reading Association.

Banks, J. A. (1973). *Teaching strategies for social studies.* Reading, MA: Addison-Wesley.

Barton, M. L. (1997). Addressing the literacy crisis: Teaching reading in the content areas. *NASSP Bulletin, 81*(587), 22–30.

Baum, S. M., Olenchak, F. R., & Owen, S. V. (1998). Gifted students with attention deficits: Fact and/or fiction? Or, can we see the forest for the trees? *Gifted Child Quarterly, 42*(2), 96–104.

Baumann, J. F. (1986). Effect of rewritten content textbook passages on middle grade students' comprehension of main ideas: Making the inconsiderate considerate. *Journal of Reading Behavior, 18*(1), 1–21.

Beach, R., & Lundell, D. (1998). Early adolescents' use of computer-mediated communication in writing and reading. In D. Reinking, M. C. McKenna, L. D. Labbo, & R. D. Kieffer (Eds.), *Handbook of literacy and technology* (pp. 93–112). Mahwah, NJ: Lawrence Erlbaum.

Bear, D. R., Templeton, S., Invernizzi, M., & Johnson, F. (1996). *Words their way: Word study for phonics, vocabulary, and spelling instruction.* Upper Saddle River, NJ: Prentice-Hall.

Beck, C., Gilles, C., O'Connor, A., & Koblitz, D. (1999). The Midwest: Life in the Mississippi River Valley. *Language Arts, 76,* 525–532.

Beck, I. L., McKeown, M. G., Hamilton, R. L., & Kucan, L. (1997). *Questioning the author: An approach for enhancing student engagement with text.* Newark, DE: International Reading Association.

Beck, I. L., McKeown, M. G., Worthy, J., Sandora, C. A., & Kucan, L. L. (1993). *Questioning the author: A year-long classroom implementation to engage students with text* (Technical Report). Pittsburgh: University of Pittsburgh, Learning Research and Development Center.

Beerens, D. R. (2000). *Evaluating teachers for professional growth: Creating a culture of motivation and learning.* Thousand Oaks, CA: Corwin.

Bereiter, C., & Scardamalia, M. (1996). Cognition and curriculum. In P. W. Jackson (Ed.), *Handbook of research on curriculum* (pp. 517–542). New York: Macmillan.

Bryant, D. P., Ugel, N., Hamff, A., & Thompson, S. (1999). Instructional strategies for content-area reading instruction. *Intervention in School and Clinic, 34,* 293–302.

Calfee, R. C., & Hiebert, E. H. (1991). Classroom assessment in reading. In R. Barr, M. Kamil, P. Rosenthal, & P. D. Pearson (Eds.), *Handbook of research on reading* (2nd ed., p. 281–309). New York: Longman.

Calkins, L. M. (1986). *The art of teaching writing.* Portsmouth, NH: Heinemann.

Carr, R. (1997). Writing a soundtrack to your life. *General Music Today, 11*(1), 21–23.

Cassady, J. K. (1998). Wordless books: No-risk tools for inclusive middle-grade classrooms. *Journal of Adolescent & Adult Literacy, 41,* 428–433.

Castagnera, E. Fisher, D., Rodifer, K., & Sax, C. (1998). *Deciding what to teach and how to teach it: Connecting students through curriculum and instruction.* Colorado Springs: PEAK Parent Center.

Cazden, C. B. (1986). Classroom discourse. In M. C. Wittrock (Ed.), *Handbook of research on teaching* (3rd ed., pp. 432–463). New York: Macmillan.

Christ, G. M. (1995). Curriculums with real-world connections. *Educational Leadership, 52*(8), 32–35.

Ciborowski, J. (1992). *Textbooks and the students who can't read them.* Cambridge, MA: Brookline.

Clay, M. (1985). *The early detection of reading difficulties* (3rd ed.). Portsmouth, NH: Heinemann.

Combs, M., & Beach, J. D. (1994). Stories and storytelling: Personalizing the social studies. *The Reading Teacher, 47,* 464–471.

Courtney, A. M., & Abodeeb, T. L. (1999). Diagnostic-reflective portfolios. *The Reading Teacher, 52,* 708–714.

Covey, S. B. (1990). *The 7 habits of highly effective people: Powerful lessons in personal change.* New York: Fireside.

Cunningham, P. M., Hall, D. P., & Defee, M. (1998). Nonability-grouped, multilevel instruction: Eight years later. *The Reading Teacher, 51,* 652–664.

Custer, R. L. (1995). Rubrics: An authentic assessment tool for technology education. *Technology Teacher, 55*(4), 27–37.

Dahl, K. L., & Farnan, N. (1998). *Children's writing: Perspectives from research*. Newark, DE: Intenational Reading Association and National Reading Conference.

Diamond, M., & Hopson, J. (1998). *Magic trees of the mind: How to nurture your child's intelligence, creativity and healthy emotions from birth through adolescence*. New York: Dutton.

Dodge, B. (1995). Webquests: A technique for Internet-based learning. *Distance Educator, 1*(2), 10–13.

Dodge, B. (1997). *Some thoughts about webquests*. (Available at: http://edweb.sdsu.edu/courses /edtec596/about_webquests.html.)

Doyle, W. (1996). Curriculum and pedagogy. In P. W. Jackson (Ed.), *Handbook of research on curriculum* (pp. 486–516). New York: Macmillan.

Dreher, M. J. (1998–1999). Motivating children to read more nonfiction. *The Reading Teacher, 52*, 414–417.

Dugan, S., & Desir, L. (1998). Ethnography and "Lucy": ESL students in the "content" class. *Research and Teaching in Developmental Education, 14*(2), 51–57.

Education Week. (1998, October 1). *Technology counts '98: Putting school technology to the test*. Bethesda, MD: Author.

Evans, R. W. (1997). Teaching social issues: Implementing an issues-centered curriculum. In E.W. Ross (Ed.), *The social studies curriculum: Purposes, problems, and possibilities* (pp. 197–212). Albany, NY: SUNY.

Faltis, C. J., & Wolfe, P. M. (Eds.). (1998). *So much to say: Adolescents, bilingualism, and ELS in the secondary school*. New York: Teachers College.

Farnan, N. (1996). Connecting adolescents and reading: Goals at the middle level. *Journal of Adolescent & Adult Literacy, 39*, 436–445.

Fisher, D., Pumpian, I., & Sax, C. (1998). High school students' attitudes about and recommendations for their peers with significant disabilities. *Journal of the Association for Persons with Severe Handicaps, 23*, 272–282.

Fisher, D., Sax, C., & Jorgensen, C. (1998). Philosophical foundations of inclusive, restructuring schools. In C. Jorgensen (Ed.), *Restructuring high schools for all students* (pp. 29–48). Baltimore: Paul H. Brookes.

Fisher, D., Sax, C., & Pumpian, I. (Eds.). (1999). *Inclusive high schools: Learning from contemporary classrooms*. Baltimore: Paul H. Brookes.

Flippo, R. F. (1997). *Reading assessment and instruction: A qualitative approach to diagnosis*. New York: Harcourt Brace.

Flood, J., & Lapp, D. (1995). Broadening the lens: Toward an expanded conceptualization of literacy. In K. A. Hinchman, D. J. Leu, & C. K. Kinzer (Eds.), *The Forty-Fourth Yearbook of the National Reading Conference* (pp. 1–16). Chicago: NRC.

Flood, J., Lapp, D., & Fisher, D. (1999). Book clubs that encourage students to examine their cultural assumptions. In S. Totten, C. Johnson, L. R. Morrow, & T. Sills-Briegel (Eds.), *Practicing what we preach: Preparing middle level educators* (pp. 261–263). New York: Falmer.

Flood, J., Lapp, D., & Wood, K. (1997). *Staff development guide*. New York: Macmillan/ McGraw-Hill.

Ford, D. Y. (1998). The underrepresentation of minority students in gifted education: Problems and promises in recruitment and retention. *Journal of Special Education, 32*, 4–14.

Freedman, R. A. (1995). The Mr. and Mrs. club: The value of collaboration in writers' workshop. *Language Arts, 72*, 97–104.

Freese, A. R. (1999). The role of reflection on preservice teachers' development in the context of a professional development school. *Teaching and Teacher Education, 15*, 895–909.

Frey, J. (1998). *Maximizing reader response through films and videos.* Unpublished master's thesis, San Diego State University, San Diego, CA.

Fry, E. B. (1969). The readability graph validated at primary levels. *The Reading Teacher, 22,* 534–538.

Gardner, H. (1999). *Intelligence reframed: Multiple intelligences for the 21st century.* New York: Basic Books.

Garner, R., & Gillingham, M. G. (1998). The Internet in the classroom: Is it the end of transmission-oriented pedagogy? In D. Reinking, M. C. McKenna, L. D. Labbo, & R. D. Kieffer (Eds.), *Handbook of literacy and technology* (pp. 221–231). Mahwah, NJ: Lawrence Erlbaum.

Goerss, B. L. (1998). Incorporating picture books into content classrooms. *Indiana Reading Journal, 30*(3), 30–35.

Goldman, S. R., & Rakestraw, J. A., Jr. (2000). Structural aspects of constructing meaning from text. In M. L. Kamil, P. B. Mosenthal, P. D. Pearson, & R. Barr (Eds.) *Handbook of reading research: Volume III* (pp. 311–335). Mahwah, NJ: Lawrence Erlbaum.

Goodman, Y. (1985). Kidwatching: Observing children in the classroom. In A. Jaggar & M. T. Smith-Burke (Eds.), *Observing the language learner* (pp. 9–18). Newark, DE: International Reading Association.

Grady, E. L. (1991). *Grady profile portfolio assessment: A performance-based assessment tool for teachers.* St. Louis: Aurbach & Associates.

Graves, D. (1983). *Writing: Teachers and children at work.* Exeter, NH: Heinemann.

Green, J. L., Harker, J. O., & Golden, J. M. (1987). Lesson construction: Differing views. In G. W. Nobblitt & W. T. Pink (Eds.), *Schooling in social context: Qualitative studies* (pp. 46–77). Norwood, NJ: Ablex.

Haas, C. (1989). Does the medium make a difference: Two studies of writing with computers. *Human Computer Interaction, 4,* 149–169.

Harp, B. (1994). *Assessment and evaluation for student centered learning.* Norwood, MA: Christopher-Gordon.

Harris, J. J., III., & Ford, D. Y. (1999). Hope deferred again: Minority students underrepresented in gifted programs. *Education and Urban Society, 31,* 225–237.

Healy, J. M. (1998, October 7). The 'meme' that ate childhood. *Education Week, 18*(6), 56, 37.

Hedberg, P. (1998). *Electronic Portfolios: Preparing the future workforce.* Unpublished master's thesis, San Diego State University, San Diego, CA.

Henkin, R. (1995). Insiders and outsiders in first-grade writing workshops: Gender and equity issues. *Language Arts, 72,* 429–434.

Hermann, B. A. (1998). Two approaches for helping poor readers become more strategic. In R. L. Allington (Ed.), *Teaching struggling readers* (pp. 168–174). Newark, DE: International Reading Association.

Hiatt, E. L., & Covington, J. (1991). Identifying and serving diverse populations. *Update on Gifted Education, 1*(3), 1–37.

Hiebert, E. H., & Frey, N. (in press). Teacher-based assessment of literacy learning. In J. Flood, J. Squire, D. Lapp, & J. Hensen (Eds.), *Handbook of Research on Teaching the English Language Arts* (2nd ed.). Mahway, NJ: Erlbaum.

Huffman, E. S. (1998). Authentic rubrics. *Art Education, 51,* 64–68.

Hunter, M. C. (1994). *Enhancing teaching.* New York: Macmillan.

Irvin, J. L., Lunstrum, J P., Lynch-Brown, C., & Shepard, M. F. (1995). *Enhancing social studies through literacy strategies.* Bulletin 91. Washington, DC: National Council for the Social Studies.

Johnson, N. M., & Ebert, M. J. (1992). Time travel is possible: Historical fiction and biography—passport to the past. *The Reading Teacher, 45,* 488–495.

Johnston, P. H., & Winograd, P. N. (1985). Passive failure in reading. *Journal of Reading Behavior, 17,* 279–301.

Jones, I., & Pellegrini, A. D. (1996). The effects of social relationships, writing media, and microgenetic development of first-grade students' written narratives. *American Educational Research Journal, 33,* 691–718.

Jorgensen, C. M. (1994). Essential questions—Inclusive answers. *Educational Leadership, 52*(4), 52–55.

Kennedy, C. H., & Fisher, D. (2001). *Inclusive middle schools.* Baltimore: Paul H. Brookes.

Kieffer, R. D., & Morrison, L. S. (1994). Changing portfolio process: One journey toward authentic assessment. *Language Arts, 71,* 411–418.

Kieffer, R. D., Hale, M. E., & Templeton, A. (1998). Electronic literacy portfolios: Technology transformations in a first-grade classroom. In D. Reinking, M. C. McKenna, L. D. Labbo, & R. D. Kieffer (Eds.), *Handbook of literacy and technology* (pp. 145–164). Mahwah, NJ: Lawrence Erlbaum.

Koretz, S. (1999). *A study of fourth grade students reading and thinking behaviors during social studies class when using multiple sources strategies.* Unpublished master's thesis, San Diego State University, San Diego, CA.

Kuhn, D. (1999). A developmental model of critical thinking. *Educational Researcher, 28*(2), 16–26.

Lapp, D., & Flood, J. (1992). *Teaching reading to every child* (3rd ed.). New York: Macmillan.

Lapp, D., Fisher, D., & Flood, J. (1999). Integrating the language arts and content areas: Effective research-based strategies. *The California Reader, 32*(4), 35–38.

Lapp, D., Fisher, D., Flood, J., & Cabello, A. (2000). An integrated approach to the teaching and assessment of language arts. In S. Hurley & J. Tinajero (Eds.), *Assessing literacy for English language learners* (pp. 1–26). Boston: Allyn & Bacon.

Lapp, D., Flood, J., & Farnan, N. (1996). *Content area reading and learning: Instructional strategies* (2nd ed.). Needham Heights, MA: Simon & Schuster.

Lapp, D., Flood, J., & Fisher, D. (1999). Intermediality: How the use of multiple media enhances learning. *The Reading Teacher, 52,* 776–780.

Lapp, D., Flood, J., & Goss, K. (2000). Desks don't move—students do: In effective classroom environments. *The Reading Teacher, 54,* 31–36.

Leitze, A. R., & Mau, S. T. (1999). Assessing problem-solving thought. *Mathematics Teaching in the Middle School, 4,* 305–311.

Lemke, J. L. (1990). *Talking science.* Norwood, NJ: Ablex.

Leslie, L., & Jett-Simpson, M. (1997). *Authentic literacy assessment: An ecological approach.* New York: Longman.

Lobach, M. R. (1995). Kids explore heritage through writer's workshop and professional publication. *The Reading Teacher, 48,* 522–524.

Macdonald, J. B., & Purpel, D. E. (1987). Curriculum and planning: Visions and metaphors. *Journal of Curriculum and Supervision, 2,* 178–192.

Martin, R. J., Van Cleaf, D. W., & Hodges, C. A. (1988). Cooperative learning: Linking reading and social studies. *Reading Psychology, 9*(1), 59–72.

Massich, M., & Munoz, E. (1996). Utilizing primary sources as building blocks for literacy. *Social Studies Review, 36*(1), 52–57.

Matanzo, J. B., & Richardson, J. S. (1998). An operatic read-aloud for music and art. *Journal of Adolescent & Adult Literacy, 41,* 490–493.

Mazzoni, S. A., & Gambrell, L. B. (1996). Text talk: Using discussion to promote comprehension of informational texts. In L. B. Gambrell & J. F. Almasi (Eds.), *Lively discussions! Fostering engaged reading* (pp. 134-148). Newark, DE: International Reading Association.

McDonnell, L. M., & McLaughlin, M. J. (1997). *Educating one and all: Students with disabilities and standards–based reform.* Washington, DC: National Academy Press.

McTighe, J., & Wiggins, G. (1999). *The understanding by design handbook.* Alexandria, VA: Association for Supervision and Curriculum Development.

Mehan, H. (1979). *Learning lessons.* Cambridge, MA: Harvard University Press.

Messaris, P. (1994). *Visual literacy: Image, mind, & reality.* Boulder, CO: Westview.

Miller, T. (1998). The place of picture books in middle-level classrooms. *Journal of Adolescent & Adult Literacy, 41,* 376–381.

Moss, B. (1991). Children's nonfiction trade books: A complement to content area texts. *The Reading Teacher, 45,* 26–32.

Mundy, J., & Hadaway, N. L. (1999). Children's informational picture books visit a secondary ESL classroom. *Journal of Adolescent & Adult Literacy, 42,* 464–475.

Nagy, W. E., & Anderson, R. C. (1984). How many words are there in printed school English? *Reading Research Quarterly, 19,* 303–330.

National Association of State Boards of Education. (1995). *Winning ways: Creating inclusive schools, classrooms, and communities.* Report of the NASBE study group on special education. Washington, DC: Author.

National Association of State Boards of Education (NASBE). (1996). *What will it take? Standards-based education for all students.* Alexandria, VA: Author.

Nieto, S. (1996). *Affirming diversity: The sociopolitical context of multicultural education* (2nd ed). White Plains, NY: Longman.

Niguidula, D. (1995). Picturing performance with digital portfolios. *Educational Leadership, 55*(3), 26–29.

Odenthal, J. M. (1992). *The effect of a computer-based writing program on the attitudes and performance of students acquiring English as a second language.* Unpublished doctoral dissertation, San Diego State University & Claremont Graduate University, San Diego, CA.

Ogle, D. M. (1986). K-W-L: A teaching model that develops active reading of expository text. *The Reading Teacher, 39,* 564–70.

Onosko, J. J., & Jorgensen, C. M. (1997). Unit and lesson planning in the inclusive classroom: Maximizing learning opportunities for all students. In C. M. Jorgensen (Ed.). *Restructuring high schools for all students: Taking inclusion to the next level* (pp. 71–106). Baltimore: Paul H. Brookes.

Owston, P. D., Murphy, S., & Wideman, H. H. (1991). On and off computer writing of eighth grade students experienced in word processing. *Computers in the Schools, 8,* 67–87.

Palincsar, A. S., & Brown, A. L. (1986). Interactive teaching to promote independent learning from text. *The Reading Teacher, 39,* 771–777.

Paris, S. (1995). *Coming to grips with authentic instruction and assessment.* Torrance, CA: Presentation sponsored by the Educational Center.

Paris, S. G., & Ayres, L. R. (1994). *Becoming reflective students and teachers with portfolios and authentic assessment.* Washington, DC: American Psychological Association.

Perry, N. E. (1998). Young children's self-regulated learning and contexts that support it. *Journal of Educational Psychology, 90,* 715–729.

Peterson, J. S., & Margolin, L. (1997). Naming gifted children: An example of unintended "reproduction." *Journal for the Education of the Gifted, 21*(1), 82–101.

Pokrywcaynski, J. (1992). *War stories can make horror stories: The characteristics students look for in a good advertising guest speaker.* Washington, DC: U.S. Department of Education.

Popham, W. J. (1999). Why standardized tests don't measure educational quality. *Educational Leadership, 56*(6), 8–15.

Posner, G. (1995). *Analyzing the curriculum* (2nd ed.). New York: McGraw-Hill.

Prain, V., & Hand, B. (1996). Writing for learning in secondary science: Rethinking practices. *Teaching and Teacher Education, 12,* 609–626.

Raphael, T. E. (1986). Teaching question-answer relationships, revisited. *The Reading Teacher, 39,* 516–522.

Raphael, T. E., Engler, C. S., & Kirschner, B. W. (1986). *The impact of text structure instruction and social context on students' comprehension and production of expository text.* (Research Series No. 177). East Lansing, MI: Michigan State University Institute for Research on Teaching.

Reinking, D. (1998). Introduction: Synthesizing technological transformations of literacy in a post-typographic world. In D. Reinking, M. C. McKenna, L. D. Labbo, & R. D. Kieffer (Eds.), *Handbook of literacy and technology* (pp. xi–xxx). Mahwah, NJ: Lawrence Erlbaum.

Richardson, J. S. (1997–1998). A read-aloud for foreign languages: Becoming a language master. *Journal of Adolescent & Adult Literacy, 41,* 312–314.

Richardson, J. S., & Gross, E. (1997). A read-aloud for mathematics. *Journal of Adolescent & Adult Literacy, 40,* 492–494.

Roach, V. (1999). Reflecting on the least restrictive environment policy: Curriculum, instruction, placement—three legs of the achievement stool. In D. Fisher, C. Sax, & I. Pumpian (Eds.), *Inclusive high schools: Learning from contemporary classrooms* (pp. 145–156). Baltimore: Paul H. Brookes.

Romanowski, M. H. (1996). Problems of bias in history textbooks. *Social Education, 60,* 170–173.

Romero, M. K. (1994). Identifying giftedness among Keresan Pueblo Indians: The Keres study. *Journal of American Indian Education, 34*(1), 35–58.

Ross, E. W. (Ed.). (1997). *The social studies curriculum: Purposes, problems, and possibilities.* Albany, NY: SUNY.

Ruddell, M. R. (1996). Engaging students' interest and willing participation in subject area learning. In D. Lapp, J. Flood, & N. Farnan (Eds.), *Content area reading and learning: Instructional strategies* (2nd ed., pp. 95–110). Boston: Allyn & Bacon.

Ruddell, M. R. H. (1991). Authentic assessment: Focused observation as a means for evaluating language and literacy development. *The California Reader, 24*(2), 2–7.

Russell, R. G. (1991, April). *A meta-analysis of word processing and attitudes and the impact on the quality of writing.* Chicago: Paper presented at the Annual Meeting of the American Educational Research Association.

Sadker, D. (1999). Gender equity: Still knocking at the door. *Educational Leadership, 56*(7), 22–26.

Santa, C. M., & Havens, L. (1995). *Creating independence through student-owned projects: Project CRISS.* Dubuque, IA: Kendall-Hunt.

Santa, C. M., Havens, L., & Harrison, S. (1996). Teaching secondary science through reading, writing, studying, and problem solving. In D. Lapp, J. Flood, & N. Farnan (Eds.), *Content area reading and learning: Instructional strategies* (2nd ed., pp. 165–179). Boston: Allyn & Bacon.

Sapon-Shevin, M. (1994a). Why gifted students belong in inclusive schools. *Educational Leadership, 52*(4), 64–68, 70.

Sapon-Shevin, M. (1994b). *Playing favorites: Gifted education and the disruption of community.* New York: State University of New York.

Saunders, W. L. (1992). The constructivist perspective: Implications and teaching strategies for science. *School Science and Mathematics, 92*(3), 136–141.

Schneider, J. J., & Jackson, S. A. W. (2000). Process drama: A special space and place for writing. *The Reading Teacher, 54,* 38–51.

Semali, L. M., & Pailliotet, A. W. (1999). *Intermediality: The teachers' handbook of critical media literacy.* Boulder, CO: Westview.

Shaver, J. P., Davis, O. L., & Helburn, S. M. (1980). An interpretive report on the status of precollege social education based on three NSF funded studies. In *What are the needs in precollege science, mathematics, and social science education? Views from the field* (pp. 3–18). Washington, DC: National Science Foundation.

Sisk, D. A. (1994). Bridging the gap between minority disadvantaged high potential children and Anglo middle class gifted children. *Gifted Education International, 10*(1), 37–43.

Slavin, R. E. (1989). Cooperative learning models for the 3 R's. *Educational Leadership, 47*(4), 22–28.

Slavin, R. E. (1995). A model of effective instruction. *Educational Forum, 59*(2), 166–176.

Spandel, V., & Stiggins, R. J. (1997). *Creating writers: Linking writing assessment and instruction* (2nd ed.). New York: Longman.

Spor, M. W., & Schneider, B. K. (1999). Content reading strategies: What teachers know, use, and want to learn. *Reading Research and Instruction, 38,* 221–231.

Squire, J. R. (1987). *Studies of textbooks: Are we asking the right questions?* Chicago: Paper presented at the Inaugural Conference of the Benton Center for Curriculum and Instruction, University of Chicago.

Stanley, J. C., & Hopkins, K. D. (1972). *Educational and psychological measurement and evaluation.* Englewood Cliffs, NJ: Prentice-Hall.

Strom, R. (1990). Talented children in minority families. *International Journal of Early Childhood, 22*(2), 39–48.

Sulzby, E. (1991). Assessment of emergent literacy: Storybook reading. *The Reading Teacher, 44,* 498–500.

Tomlinson, C. A. (1999). *The differentiated classroom: Responding to the needs of all learners.* Alexandria, VA: Association for Supervision and Curriculum Development.

Towell, J. H. (1999–2000). Motivating students through music and literature. *The Reading Teacher, 53,* 284–287.

Tucker, M. S., & Codding, J. B. (1998). *Standards for our schools: How to set them, measure them, and reach them.* San Francisco: Jossey-Bass.

Tunnell, M. O., & Ammon, R. (1996). The story of ourselves: Fostering multiple historical perspectives. *Social Education, 57,* 224–225.

U.S. Department of Education. (1999). *To assure the free appropriate public education of all children with disabilities (IDEA, Section 618).* Twenty-first annual report to Congress on the implementation of the Individuals with Disabilities Education Act. Washington, DC: Author.

Vacca, R. T., Vacca, J. L., Prosenjak, N., & Burkey, L. (1996). Creating response-centered learning environments. In D. Lapp, J. Flood, & N. Farnan (Eds.), *Content area reading and learning: Instructional strategies* (2nd ed., pp. 355–367). Boston: Allyn & Bacon.

Valencia, S. W., Hiebert, E. H., & Afflerbach, P. P. (1994). *Authentic reading assessment: Practices and possibilities.* Newark, DE: International Reading Association.

Vygotsky, L. S. (1978). *Mind in society: The development of higher psychological processes.* Cambridge: MA: Harvard University Press.

Watts-Taffe, S., & Truscott, D. M. (2000). Using what we know about language and literacy development for ESL students in the mainstream classroom. *Language Arts, 77,* 258–265.

West, G. B. (1978). *Teaching reading skills in content areas: A practical guide to the construction of student exercises* (2nd ed.). Oviedo, FL: Sandpiper.

West, K. R. (1998). Noticing and responding to learners: Literacy evaluation and instruction in the primary grades. *The Reading Teacher, 51,* 550–559.

Wilcox, B. L. (1997). Writing portfolios: Active vs. passive. *English Journal, 86*(6), 34–37.

Wilkinson, L. C., & Silliman, E. R. (2000). Classroom language and literacy learning. In M. L. Kamil, P. B. Mosenthal, P. D. Pearson, & R. Barr (Eds.) *Handbook of reading research: Volume III* (pp. 311–335). Mahwah, NJ: Lawrence Erlbaum.

Winograd, P., & Paris, S. G. (1989). A cognitive and motivational agenda for reading instruction. *Educational Leadership, 46*(4), 30–36.

Woodward, A., Elliott, D. L., & Nagel, K. C. (1986). Beyond textbooks in elementary social studies. *Social Education, 50,* 50–53.

Worthy, J., & Hoffman, J. V. (1999). Critical questions. *The Reading Teacher, 52,* 520–521.

Wortmann, G. B. (1992). An invitation to learning. *Science Teacher, 59*(2), 19–22.

Yancey, K. B. (1992). *Portfolios in the writing classroom.* Urbana, IL: National Council of Teachers of English.

Yell, M. L., Rogers, D., & Rogers, E. L. (1998). The legal history of special education: What a long, strange trip it's been! *Remedial and Special Education, 19,* 219–228.

Books Cited

Addy, S. H. (1999). *Right here on this spot.* New York: Houghton Mifflin.

Boas, J. (1996). *We are witnesses: Five diaries of teenagers who died in the Holocaust.* New York: Scholastic.

Brodksy, J. (1999). *Discovery.* New York: Farrar Straus Giroux.

Coerr, E. (1999). *Sadako.* New York: Puffin.

Cushman, K. (1995). *Catherine, called Birdy.* New York: Harper Trophy.

Cushman, K. (2000). *Matilda bone.* New York: Clarion.

David, R. (1993). *Growing up in ancient Egypt.* Mahwah, NJ: Troll.

De Angeli, M. (1989). *The door in the wall.* New York: Doubleday.

Denenberg, B. (1997). *Voices from Vietnam.* New York: Scholastic.

Douglass, F. (1994). *Escape from slavery: The boyhood of Frederick Douglass in his own words.* New York: Knopf.

Filipovic, Z. (1995). *Zlata's Diary: A Child's Life in Sarajevo.* New York: Penguin.

Fleishman, P. (1988). *Joyful Noise: Poems for two voices.* New York: HarperCollins.

Fradin, D. (1984). *Explorers.* New York: Children's Press.

Frank, A., & Mooyaart, B. M. (1993). *Anne Frank: The diary of a young girl.* New York: Bantam.

Garland, S. (1995). *The silent storm.* New York: Harcourt Brace.

Garland, S. (1997). *The lotus seed.* New York: Voyager.

Giblin, J. (2000). *The amazing life of Benjamin Franklin*. New York: Scholastic.

Gollub, M. (1998). *Cool melons-turn to frogs! The life and poems of Issa*. New York: Lee & Low.

Huynh, S. T. (1996). *An anthology of Vietnamese poems: From the eleventh through the twentieth centuries*. New Haven, CT: Yale.

Jimenez, F. (1996). *The circuit*. New York: Houghton Mifflin.

Knight, M. B. (1993). *Who belongs here? An American story*. Gardiner, ME: Tilbury.

Kodama, T. (1995). *Shin's tricycle*. New York: Walker.

Kramer, S. (1997). *Eye of the storm: Chasing storms with Warren Faidley*. New York: Putnam.

Krull, K. (1993). *Lives of the musicians: Good times, bad times (and what the neighbors thought)*. San Diego: Harcourt Brace.

Langley, A., Dann, G. & Brightling, G. (2000). *Eyewitness: Medieval life*. New York: DK Publishing.

Lowry, L. (1989). *Number the stars*. New York: Houghton Mifflin.

MacDonald, F. (1997). *How would you survive in the Middle Ages?* New York: Franklin Watts.

MacDonald, F. (1999). *Women in ancient Egypt: Other half of history*. Lincolnwood, IL: Peter Bedrick.

McKay, L. (1998). *Journey home*. New York: Lee & Low.

Moerbeek, K., & Dijs, C. (1997). *Six brave explorers: A pop-up book*. Pensacola, FL: Presto Print.

Montgomery, J., & Hinson, M. (1995). *Meet the great composers*. Van Nuys, CA: Alfred.

Paulsen, G. (1999). *My life in dog years*. New York: Yearling.

Pickney, A. D. (1998). *Dear Benjamin Banneker*. New York: Voyager.

Prelutsky, J. (1996). *Pizza the size of the sun: Poems by Jack Prelutsky*. New York: Greenwillow.

Pyle, H. (1967). *Otto of the silver hand*. Mineola, NY: Dover.

Rice, E. (2000). *Life during the Middle Ages: The way people live*. New York: Lucent.

Robertson, B. (1999). *Marguerite makes a book*. Los Angeles: J. Paul Getty Museum.

Roop, C. (1999). *Girl of the shining mountains: Sacagawea's story*. New York: Hyperion.

Sandburg, C. (1995). *Poetry for young people*. New York: Sterling.

Shepard, A. (1998). *The crystal heart: A Vietnamese legend*. New York: Atheneum.

Sis, P. (1996). *Follow the dream*. New York: Dragonfly.

Soto, G. (1996). *Canto familiar*. San Diego, CA: Harcourt Brace.

Spinelli, J. (1998). *Knots in my yo-yo string: The autobiography of a kid*. New York: Knopf.

Spivak, D. (1997). *Grass sandals: The travels of Basho*. New York: Atheneum.

Stewart, A. (2000). *Keeping clean: Everyday history*. New York: Franklin Watts.

Tanaka, S. (1996). *Anastasia's album*. New York: Hyperion.

Tsuchiya, Y. (1951). *Faithful elephants: A true story of animals, people and war*. Boston: Houghton Mifflin.

Uchida, Y. (1995). *The invisible thread: An autobiography*. New York: Beech Tree.

Vining, E. G. (1987). *Adam of the road*. New York: Viking.

Whelan, G. (1993). *Goodbye, Vietnam*. New York: Random House.

Winter, J. (1999). *Sebastian: A book about Bach*. San Diego: Harcourt Brace.

ABOUT THE AUTHORS

Douglas Fisher and Nancy Frey are faculty members in teacher education at San Diego State University. In addition, they coordinate the professional development school efforts at Rosa Parks Elementary, Monroe Clark Middle, and Hoover High Schools. They are interested in urban education, student achievement, and planning curriculum and instruction for all students. They can be reached at dfisher@mail.sdsu.edu and nfrey@mail.sdsu.edu, respectively.